Railroad Management

Railroad Management

D. Daryl Wyckoff
Harvard University

Lexington Books
D.C. Heath and Company
Lexington, Massachusetts
Toronto   London

Library of Congress Cataloging in Publication Data

Wyckoff, D. Daryl.
  Railroad management.

  Bibliography: p.
  Includes index.
  1. Railroads — Management. 2. Railroads — United States.
I. Title.
HE1626.W93   658'.91'385   75-5237
ISBN 0-669-99770-6

Copyright © 1976 by D.C. Heath and Company

Published simultaneously in Canada

Printed in the United States of America

International Standard Book Number: 0-669-99770-6

Library of Congress Catalog Card Number: 75-5237

To Charles Mitchell Hammer
of the Kansas City, Mexico, and
Orient Railway and the Atchison,
Topeka, and Santa Fe Railway: a
little-known but dedicated
railroader, and my grandfather.

Contents

List of Figures

List of Tables

Preface

Two things encouraged me to research and write this book. First, I have great concern for the future of American railroads, which goes well beyond my nostalgic, personal interest as an individual with a family tradition in railroading. My greater concern is for the loss of an important private-sector industry and its capacity as an important contributor to our economy. Second, I found that several individuals were attempting to apply my previous research and findings regarding organizational behavior and structure in the motor carrier industry to the railroad industry. Although the objective of reexamining organizational behaviors and structures of railroads was appropriate, I was concerned that the application of motor carrier findings to railroads was not.

I wrote this book for the decision makers who may most influence the future of railroads: managers, investors, shippers, regulators, and legislators. As the railroads have progressed in their path of collapse, a greater number of individuals outside the railroad industry have become involved in the determination of its future. I hope that this work will contribute to the understanding of this industry for these people.

However, my greatest concern is for the railroad managers. As the railroads have failed, this group has been highly criticized. The general public holds the opinion that if there were better managers at the helms of the railroads, the present unfortunate state of the industry would not exist. I do not excuse these managers from responsibility for the situation, but I think they have been maligned. The present railroad situation was set largely by events that occurred several decades ago, well before the tenure of most current railroad managers. In addition, constraints on freedom of action by management have been added by outside forces with each passing year.

There is as much latent management ability and sincere desire for a healthy industry in railroads as in most other sectors of business. Nevertheless, the performance has been disappointing. It is too simplistic to say that railroads cannot be managed because too many constraints have been placed on management; many of these constraints are the direct and indirect results of errors of omission and commission by past and present railroad managers. But the best managers from some of the most successful sectors of business might have little if any more success in managing the railroads without some relaxation of these constraints and two other important actions: (1) restoration to all levels of railroad management of a new vigor and the belief that success is possible, and (2) development throughout the companies of a new spirit of integration or balance in the individual functional areas (particularly operations and marketing).

The most damaging constraint placed on railroad management is self-imposed. Railroad managers accept current organization structure, balance of power, and management style as givens. As one high-ranking railroad officer commented when I raised questions in these areas, "I thought we settled that years ago." He is right, and he is wrong. For too many managers, acceptance of practices of management and organizations that are decades old (some dating from the early 1900s) does settle the issue. But, a great deal has changed that should cause constant reexamination and revision of these key strategic issues.

Are railroad managers different? Or are they simply the product of the bureaucratic institutions in which they operate? If their parochial functional behavior and submissive attitude are products of the institutions, and are not the results of basic personal incompetence, can the institutions be changed? Or, are the privately owned, independent railroads past the point of no return? If so, then the matter *was* settled years ago, and we must look for other actions.

While the subject of this book is railroad management, the theme is contingency management. That is, there is no one universal organization structure appropriate for all situations. Rather, the appropriate organization for an enterprise in any particular situation is contingent on several factors, including the objectives; management tasks; competitive, market, technological and regulatory environment; traditions and history; and personal abilities and desires of the individuals.

The railroad situation is incredibly difficult because of the magnitude of the momentum of years of rigidity in practice, reinforcement of behavior, on-the-job training, and large number of participants. But, I conclude this study on a note of constrained optimism. There is evidence of increasing vigor and integration in several railroads. These successful breaks with tradition are encouraging. There is, then, evidence that the cause is not hopeless.

If this book in any way encourages railroad managers to reexamine their organizations and management styles, I will consider it successful. My intention is to provide a conceptual framework and path for those who are willing to accept this challenge.

Acknowledgments

This work was made possible by several hundred people who contributed their time and insights to the project. My objective was to gain a fresh view of the railroad industry that would help its managers better understand the context in which they were operating. The railroad industry is historical and full of tradition and conventional wisdom. My task was to pierce this and to find new meanings, seeking new alternatives for management. It required many hours of discussion to penetrate this veneer with hundreds of interview hours, scores of computer hours for processing questionnaires and operating data, and many thousands of miles of travel. My sense of mission drove me on, but the faith of those who contributed to this work in various ways amazed me. Unfortunately, it is impossible to mention each person here.

My interest in railroading and railroad management has existed for many years. However, the individual who most encouraged me to undertake this study was A. Scheffer Lang of the Association of American Railroads. It was his concern for the tasks of railroad management and our discussions about my earlier works examining the motor carrier management that led directly to this work. Another who made special contributions to challenge my thinking was Alfred E. Perlman; the days we spent discussing railroading are very dear to me.

Hundreds of people completed questionnaires. The response to this request was outstanding. Also, many of my railroad students in the Harvard Business School Advanced Management Program and Program for Management Development were loyal critics of my early drafts. William R. Martin and William B. Fleisher of the Staff Studies Group of the Office of the President of the Association of American Railroads made important contributions to my technical knowledge of the industry and served as consulting critics.

I wish to extend special thanks to: David Hughes and Michael V. Smith of the Boston and Maine; John W. Barriger, J.G. Hardin, A.L. Lawson, and D.G. Ruegg of the Atchison, Topeka and Santa Fe; R.G. (Mike) Flanery of the Western Pacific; Denman K. McNear and William Settle of Southern Pacific Transportation; Rome Blair and J.E. Gregg of the Kansas City Southern; Joseph F. Folk of the Penn Central; and James R. Lynch, H.S. Meislahn, and J.C. Humbert of the Illinois Central Gulf. While many contributed to my insights in the industry, these people made special contributions. The Southern Railway System became a subject of special attention in my research. I worked with many people there, but I particularly wish to thank: W. Graham Claytor, Jr., L. Stanley Crane, Harold H. Hall, Robert S. Hamilton, R.D. Hedberg, John L. Jones, Frank L. Luckett, George S. Paul, and Walter W. Simpson.

I also wish to thank my faculty colleagues at the Harvard Business School, in particular, Alexander L. Morton, Cyrus F. Gibson, and J.W. Lorsch. The Harvard Graduate School of Business Administration with Dean Lawrence Fouraker, the Division of Research, and the 1907 Foundation provided the resources and a challenging environment of transportation research.

This book is dedicated to Charles Mitchell Hammer, my grandfather. He was the first railroader I ever knew and it is his love of railroading that started me on this present path.

Finally, I wish to thank my family for their support and understanding during this project: thank you Valerie, Michele, and Abigail.

While I gratefully acknowledge the many sources of help and guidance in the preparation of this book, I fully accept the responsibility for the findings, conclusions, and all technical or mechanical aspects of the work.

Railroad Management

1 Introduction

Railroads in the United States have failed to pursue the aggressive organizational change and innovation that is necessary to prepare them for today's management tasks. The next several years will see either a major change in their abilities to cope with their environments in order to prosper from available opportunities, or a continued progression of failures that lead to the collapse of the private-sector railroad concept.

The viability of the privately owned and operated railroad in the United States is being seriously challenged. Within the next decade we may well know the results of this challenge. As one who believes in the value of such a private-sector industry, it is my desire that this book's analysis of railroad management may contribute to a better understanding of several courses of action open to management for averting the complete breakdown of the system.

I concentrate here on the issue of organization and management structure as a key variable still within the perogative of railroad managers. By *organization* and *management structure* I mean the composite of formal and informal relationships of individual parts of the company to each other—how the company is organized to deal with the task of achieving its corporate objectives. I subscribe to the contingency theory of management, which states that the most effective or appropriate organization is one that is uniquely suited to and contingent upon the tasks of the firm, the environment in which it operates, and the predispositions and resources of its members.[1] This is the opposite of the classicists' view of organizational behavior, which sought universal solutions to organizational design problems: one organization for all situations. I believe that there is not only the problem of designing an appropriate organization for the railroad industry, but it is necessary to design an organization for each railroad's unique situation. The members of the railroad industry have too long failed to reevaluate aggressively whether their organizations are appropriate for their industry generally and (more importantly) for their companies specifically.

Why concentrate on organization in an industry so overwhelmed with problems, many of which are outside the hands of managers? I certainly grant that the current state of the industry may be laid to: (1) fluctuations

1

between overzealous and sluggish regulation, (2) restrictive labor practices and rules, (3) government subsidy and encouragement of competitive modes, and (4) incompetent and/or unscrupulous (or greedy) management. Obviously different observers, depending on their own background, vantage point, and stake in the situation, are likely to have different views.

I acknowledge the importance of each of these issues in examining the management tasks of railroads as business enterprises and the appropriateness of the present railroad management structures to accomplish them. However, while there may be some varying degree of validity in each of the potential causes stated above, I believe that too much blame has been heaped on them by those who seek simplistic explanations of the problems. I question the idea that accepting the recommendations that are frequently offered on these four points will solve the problem. Eliminating the ICC, eliminating the maze of work rules imposed by the unions, halting the construction of highways, or imposing more restrictive operating restrictions on trucks will not bring the railroads to full health, although these might be very invigorating steps. As in many companies in other industries, there are some candidates for replacement by better trained, more vigorous, and more intelligent managers. But, wholesale replacement of the managers of the industry may not be practical, necessary, or desirable.

The first three and perhaps the fourth points mentioned above are largely outside the hands of the present managers. The most frustrating part of the task of railroad management, based on my interviews and discussions with managers, is the sense of inability to make direct impact on the situation. Yet, one of the vital ingredients of the ensemble of management tools is organization.

This option, which is largely in the hands of managers rather than outside institutions, has been unexercised for too long. In fact, the organizational failures may have led to a management stance that in turn led the railroads into the present situations on the points listed above.

Above all, I condemn the tendency of railroad managers to be overdependent on tradition and conventional wisdom in an industry where greater adaptability to the environment is possible.

It might be justified that issues of regulation, labor practices, and competitive development were not in the direct control of the railroad managers. Certainly, great amounts of energy have been allocated to these issues by railroad managers to little effect. The efforts to attack or respond to these points might have been directed in more effective ways. But if these changes in the environment could not have been halted, what could railroad managers have done to minimize their impact or capitalize on the opportunities?

Major Objective of Railroads' Organizations and the "Chinese Wall" Barriers

If the railroads may be faulted as an industry for failure, I agree with the majority of railroad managers, railroad customers, and government observers who believe that this fault is the inability of the railroads to develop and to pursue vigorously an integrated operating, marketing, and financial strategy. Referred to as the "Chinese Walls of Management," the functional groups of a railroad tend to operate with little integration of activities toward a common purpose except in the executive office. In fact, this jealously guarded differentiation is so strong that I even observed a strong sense of rivalry between functional areas on some properties.

A recent survey I made of railroad managers at different levels in their functional organizations provided some interesting insights. When railroad managers were asked what were the most important tasks that their railroads faced, the answers fit a very clear pattern. First, there was a high occurrence of answers indicating greater cooperation between commercial and operating functions, mostly by commercial function managers. But, this in itself was not overwhelming. The next most frequent answer was that the opposite functional group from the group of the respondent had to improve to support the respondent's group better, and the third highest response was that the respondent's functional group should be given resources to improve the performance of this group (presumably at the disadvantage of the opposite functional group).

While I would hesitate to claim statistical reliability for the sample, these managers showed three unattractive features of the monolithic functional organizations of which they were members: First, some perceived a need for greater integration of the functions. The recognition of the problem is commendable; the existence of the problem is not. Second, there was evidence of parochial functional interest. Third, there was a suspicion of and a lack of appreciation for the legitimacy of the constraints placed on their functional group by the opposite group.

The second feature of railroad management organizations that might be examined is the growing tendency toward centralization. As the computer has become more highly developed, the long-time dream of railroad managers of controlling a carefully optimized railroad system appears to be more practical. But, even if increased capitalization is becoming more practical, is it desirable if it stifles the vigor of local management?

Nineteenth-century Sources of Functional Organization

Why are railroads organized as they are? All of the railroads in the United States are organized in essentially the same way, with two minor variations, which I refer to as Type I and Type II. These forms date from the late nineteenth century.

The Type I organization, as shown in figure 1-1, is basically a strict departmental structure, where line authority flows from the chief officer of a functional department directly to the field group without significant integration with other departments at less than the executive level. The Type II organization integrates all operating departments on a regional (or geographical divisional) basis. Under such an organization, the regional maintenance of way officer is responsible to the regional operations officer (usually called a division superintendent) for repair of track and structures, but receives *staff* direction in matters pertaining to standards and practices from the chief officer of maintenance of way and structures. In a similar way, other regional operating officers have line responsibility to the regional manager and staff relationships to their respective chief officers. In some cases, several geographic divisions may report to a general superintendent in extremely large organizations. There are some rare cases of hybrid organizations in which some operating functions are regionalized (or divisionalized) and other functions retain the departmental relationship more typical of the Type I organization. The Type II organization, as might be expected, is more often found on large railroads, but this is not necessarily true. While geography might suggest a tendency towards a particular structure, the tradition of the individual company is often much more the determinant of the structure.

From the above, particularly if one had not been exposed to a variety of organizations outside of the railroad industry, there might be a tendency to conclude that there is substantial diversity in railroad organizational structures. However, I would suggest the opposite. First, most American railroads are organized as Type II structures. Second, the differences in the Type I and Type II structures are not as great as might be imagined, since they center around the level and degree of integration or differentiation of only the operating functions of the company.

Of course, from figure 1-1 it is easily observed that there would be a natural tendency for operating and commercial or marketing functions to be isolated from each other.

As one who supports the contingency theory of management and believes that environment, strategy, and organization should be related, I would look to the environment and strategies of the early railroads for the determinants of the development of the organization.

When the present form of railroad management organization evolved, the companies were considerably smaller in size (in geography, system mileage, and employment), faced less intermodal competition, had fewer technological innovations (particularly in the communications area), and had been less exposed to diverse, alternative forms of organization.

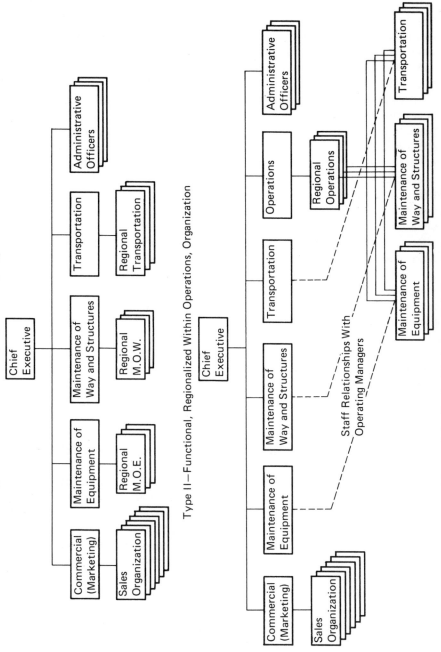

Figure 1-1. Basic Variants of Railroad Organizations

The main task of the railroad was operation. The primary task of marketing, if one were to describe the commercial function of the period in those terms, was to determine "what the traffic would bear." The organizational designs of United States railroads of the late nineteenth century stressed decentralized attention to controlling and moving trains in a coordinated and consistent fashion that is within the dictates of the "rules of the road."

As intermodal competition developed, it became increasingly more necessary to refine and modify the product (services) to fit the marketplace better. However, the commercial function, which has tended to be subordinate to the operating function in seniority and social ranking, was given the task of primarily selling what operations elected to produce. Of course, this was partially justified by the massive investment and momentum of the physical plant and operations of a railroad. However, it was also rationalized by many with sound justification, that since the shipper's decision or "sale" was often made at a point other than where the operations were performed, there was good cause for these functions to be separated organizationally as well as geographically.

Also, there were inherent problems of allocation of joint costs with the joint products of a railroad. Even if it were possible to match costs with revenues, it was generally believed that it was extremely difficult to relate the two to the responsible individual.

Twentieth-century Solidification

As the railroad industry entered the twentieth century, the now familiar patterns of large organizations in maturing industries began to appear. Railroad organizations became massive and management became diffused among an army of individuals of lesser ability at the lower levels of the bureaucratic structures. As employment leveled and opportunities for rapid promotion dwindled, a system of advancement by seniority developed. Initiative and vigor were replaced by on-the-job apprentice-master training, greater security in rules, and patience. Because of the large-system nature of the railroads, the input of one person in the system was difficult to identify with a discrete and recognizable output. But breaking a rule or acting in a way that is outside the social constraints could be immediately spotted and punished. Also, as traditions of functional organizations continued over the years in increasingly larger firms, the likelihood of a young manager gaining or holding a meaningful appreciation or sympathy for the viewpoint or problems of the other functional groups was small. Functional specialization, not general management across functional lines, was desired and its development was rewarded by promotion.

This pattern of development has several implications. It is well known and recognized by potential employment candidates who consider joining railroads. It leads to a self-selective process in which candidates with tendencies for less vigor and greater desire for security are more likely to be attracted to railroads. These patterns are reinforced by the organization, together with an emphasis on functional specialization. The result is a tendency of the members of the organization to reinforce its values by personal preference and a very questionable preparation for any other type of situation.

Increasing Centralization

Concurrent with the solidification of the functional organization, there has been a tendency toward an increasing degree of control to be exercised by central organizations in railroads. The development of improved rapid communications and the computer have been instrumental in this. The railroads were among the earliest users of nearly every communication and data processing innovation. The geographic dispersion of the railroads certainly encouraged the former, and the volume of transactions of the railroads promoted the latter.

However, the adoption of these innovations might have led to greater independence of the decentralized local operating and commercial units. Instead, there has been the opposite result in almost every firm and a general weakening of the local situation. From my interviews with railroad managers, I would suspect that it is the result of two factors. First, railroads are highly systemic, and there is a great temptation to seek system optimization through centralization of control under a "master-mind" organization. Second, I have detected a marked distrust of field managers by many railroad executives. At times this almost reaches a demeaning attitude. This may stem from a basic insecurity among the executives who remember the sense of hopelessness they felt as junior managers relative to the massiveness of the system. Whether it is because of this or other reasons, I observed a strong tendency towards favoring technocratic rather than interpersonal behavior solutions. I have found a profound belief and faith in Norbert-Wiener-like cybernetics in more than one railroad executive.

The implication of this increased centralization appears to be a reduced ability of railroads to deal with local operations in a vigorous manner. The greater the degree of transactional orientation on a railroad (contrasted to the movement focus of a long-haul, run-through railroad), the higher the proportion of its revenue is spent in transportation expenses as the volume of transactions (carloads per year) and the geographical dispersion (system miles) increase. Movement-oriented railroads appear better able to bury this problem in their business, and small transaction railroads appear to be better able to keep it under control with conventional organizations. But, the large, transactionally oriented railroad is unable to cover it.

Possible Courses of Action

So, there are substantial forces that tend to reinforce the conventional railroad management organizations and the behavior seen in them. The traditions of a period when control of operations was the primary task of management, when commercial functions were of secondary significance, are still powerful. The solidification of values and employee development provide strong reinforcement to earlier organizational and social structure and produce managers who are ill-prepared for integrative management either by training or personality. The process itself is a complex system in which it is difficult to identify the impact of specific actions or individual managers. This has discouraged control or incentive systems, which attempt to identify the revenues and costs of specific activities as profit centers at a level below that of the firm itself, now familiar in many other industries. Innovation in communications and data processing have been employed to reinforce rather than counteract these previous tendencies, often further reducing the role of the local manager. Now, in the last quarter of the twentieth century, we find that the railroad industry has evolved into a relatively inflexible and traditionally solidified pattern of management organizations and behavior, (partially) from the preference of its managers, but more from the inherent technology and joint-cost nature of the industry and historical accident.

The question is, can this progression of development be broken? Or, are the attitudes, traditions, technologies so strong and the resources so depleted that it is impossible at this stage?

This book considers these forces in detail with the purpose of evaluating the probable scenarios of alternative courses of action, which might include:

1. Decentralize the organizations of existing railroads around profit centers.

2. Reconfigure existing large railroads into smaller railroads that can be effectively managed by existing organizations and managers by breaking up present railroads or separating track ownership and operating companies.

3. Minimize local operating and commercial functions by developing railroads as wholesalers of intercity transportation, abdicating local operations to other institutions.

4. Minimize need for local management of operating functions by accelerated development of and investment in communications and data processing innovations.
5. Restructure railroad properties so as to submerge the intense local operations problems of short-haul operations into railroads with predominantly more of the easily managed and profitable long-haul operations.
6. Accept existing management organizations and "force" integrative behavior by means other than decentralized profit centers.

While several of the alternatives above have little practical probability of being successful, any of them is probably preferable and more practical than the alternative of nationalization. Besides the arguments against nationalization of the railroads being the employer of last resort, being unable to discontinue unnecessary services, and political dominations, I would add another argument: nationalization of the railroads in the United States, as in all other countries where it has occurred, will reinforce the management organization and behavior of the past. In the large, nationalized railroads I have studied, centralized, functional organizations have been retained and even strengthened to ill effect.

The task here is not to find reasons why integration at all levels of the railroad cannot be achieved; rather, it is to search for ways to achieve it, given the constraints of the environment, technology, and the past.

Notes

1. See: Alfred D. Chandler, Jr., *Strategy and Structure* (Garden City, New York: Doubleday and Co., Inc., 1966). Also, Paul Lawrence and Jay Lorsch, *Organization and Environment*, (Boston: Harvard Business School, 1967).

2 Contingency Organization Theory

Jay Lorsch of the Harvard Business School defines *contingency theory* as "a way of thinking (a conceptual map) which argues that the characteristics of effective organization and effective leadership behavior in such organizations are contingent upon the situational context in which the organization exists."[1] Lorsch defines organization as the composite of formal and informal relationships of the individual parts of the company to each other. By *effective*, Lorsch is specifically referring to an organization that is achieving its purpose.

Similarly, in the 1960s, Alfred Chandler argued that the organizational structure of the firm follows its strategy.[2] But, pressing Chandler's argument slightly further, strategy and structure are highly related in successful firms. A change in structure or organization may stem from the strategic decisions of a firm to change the way it copes with its environment and the technology of its operations. However, it has been equally well argued that the structure of the organization may seriously restrict the strategic options considered by the firm's management. So, while I agree with Chandler's original proposition that structure follows strategy, I believe he would agree with my modification of this statement that strategy may follow structure, or at least be constrained by it.

In summary, regardless which statement of the theory most clearly describes it, I would agree with Lorsch in his conclusion that the search for a universal, one-best way to manage, organize, and compensate for all situations is off. Rather, the issue is to design a management organization that is appropriate for the situation of a specific company situation.[3] The descriptors of the situation are, as a minimum: (1) operating, competitive, regulatory, marketing, and labor environment; (2) industry setting (including the relative degree of intraindustry cooperation and competition); (3) financial and other resources; (4) technology and other operating features; (5) managerial resources and expectations; and (6) history and traditions.

Similarity of Response of an Industry

It is considerably more likely that firms in one industry are responding to a similar set of situational conditions in the same way as firms outside the

11

industry. Following this line of reasoning, it is relatively easy to identify features of the "industry situation," which all railroads experience, that would suggest there would be a high degree of similarities in strategies and management organizations.[a]

All United States railroads face similar regulatory environments. While specific railroads may have unique problems in some communities or states, they are all regulated by the Interstate Commerce Commission in a similar way.

Also, nearly every railroad in the United States is faced with similar labor environments. The few exceptions to this are quite notable, and substantially different strategies and organizations have developed in these situations.

The technologies of individual railroad operations are basically similar. While some roads may have opted for one producer of data processing equipment over another or for electrified locomotives over diesel, these differences do not appreciably change the management task.

Each individual railroad finds itself in somewhat different settings relative to the extent that it is in competition with other railroads or dependent upon them to originate, terminate, or pass through vital traffic. For example, the Western Pacific Railroad is vitally dependent on its relations with connecting railroads since it originates approximately 35 percent of the traffic it carries. It is reasonable that this point would be a serious determinant of the nature of its operating and marketing strategies and organizations. Similarly, a railroad such as the Penn Central, which competes with other railroads on so many fronts as a "retailer" railroad, certainly has different problems than the "wholesaler" bridge railroad or the isolated railroad.

But, the greatest competition is more frequently intermodal. Depending on the geographical setting and the nature of the commodities shipped in the markets served, a railroad may find itself in a high to very high competitive situation. This depends on the location of the railroad to waterways and interstate highways, and this in turn may depend on decisions of the federal government relative to regional development expenditures. Certainly, the degree of intensity of this intermodal competition is a major determinant of strategy and organization.

It is obvious that the physical operating environments of different railroads are quite dissimilar. The heavy, industrialized, urbanized Northeast is quite different from the more rural and more climatically favorable Southeast or the open territory of the far West.

The histories of individual railroads are different and have led to different resources (financial, mineral, real estate, etc.) at this stage in their

[a] The argument for industrywide responses is made in Joan Woodward, *Management and Technology* (London: Her Majesty's Printing Office, 1958).

development. Similarly, the histories of individual railroads have led to different traditions and expectations of their managers, customers, and lenders.

Finally, individual railroads have substantially different geographical dispersions and levels of volume of business. It has been demonstrated by studies in another transportation industry that the most effective organization was highly contingent on the number of locations served and the volume of transactions.[4]

So, if one looks at the striking similarities of the regulatory and labor environments, the similarities in technologies and joint-costing and joint-product nature of the railroad process, it is relatively easy to conclude that the strategies and structures of the entire industry are likely to be similar. However, this must be accepted in face of the strong dissimilarities among firms in competitive and operating environments and historical traditions, management expectations, and resources. Can it really be true that these differences are so insignificant relative to the intraindustry similarities that no appreciable differences in management organization of the individual railroads would exist?

Integration and Differentiation

One of the most important features of organizational design that may be exercised in contingency theory is the extent to which integration or differentiation occurs at various levels of the firm.

Differentiation in an organization has been defined by Paul R. Lawrence and Jay W. Lorsch as differences in attitude and behavior as well as segmentation by specialized knowledge and skills.[5] A more operationally oriented definition might be a high degree of specialization (such as marketing department differentiated from operations department) in jobs and orientation toward particular goals. Lawrence and Lorsch pointed out that these differences in orientation may include dissimilar time, cognitive, emotional, and interpersonal orientations.

Integration is defined by Lawrence and Lorsch as the quality of the state of collaboration that exists among departments that are required to achieve unity of effort by the demands of the environment. In other words, integration refers to a high state of interdepartmental relations or the process by which this state is achieved.[6] Similarly, an integrator is an individual who resolves interdepartmental conflicts and facilitates unified decision making.

This is not simply the matter of an operating expert becoming more tolerant of the marketing expert who is naive in operations, and vice versa. Nor is it just a marketing manager "taking an operating manager out to lunch." It is accepting other orientations and internalizing them in your own considerations. Integration is true collaboration among people with different kinds of expertise who have differentiated perspectives on the work of the organization, face different problems, and command different resources.

The key to successful integration is conflict resolution, and this in itself is not a natural process. In fact, the first order economic rewards to division of labor and specialization tend to be driving forces to frustrate integration. Much of the task of "general management" is to achieve the advantages of unified strategy and harmony of integration without appreciable loss of the advantages of differentiation.

There are several ways to achieve integration. Committees are certainly one means of achieving integration, but with a potentially serious loss of decisiveness, speed of response, and high cost.[7] Some other companies now have individuals who are outside of the conventional functional organization who are designated as integrators. Examples of these are the product managers of companies such as the IBM Corporation or Du-Pont. The most classic approach is the "shared boss," working on the assumption that such an individual has the authority to resolve conflicts and evaluate trade-offs among his subordinates.[8]

Regardless of where this integration is to take place in the organization, its success appears to be dependent on the following conditions: The integrator must be recognized as having an important voice in the decision. He must be respected by the others as highly competent and must be able to relate this expertise to the decision at hand in a way that is perceived as objective and fair. This also implies that the integrator is in a position to see clearly the implications of decisions and the specific trade-offs. This is often considered to be at the level in the organization at which a meaningful profit center can be effectively established. Finally, the integrator is generally most effective when those to be "integrated" are roughly on parity in terms of status and influence in the group.[9]

Integration in Railroad Organizations

There have been several attempts to achieve integration in railroad organizations at points lower than the executive office; however, with very few exceptions these attempts have fallen short of the desired objectives. Without cataloging the individual situations, the following are the general causes for these failures.

The most popular attempt at integration undertaken by several railroads was the market or industry-manager approach. The industry manager was to be an integrator standing between the conventional commercial and operating organizations. He was to become the expert on a specific industry (usually without geographical boundaries) and integrate the efforts of the company's functional organizations to best respond to that market's special demands.[b]

The results of these industry integrators have typically fallen short of expectations. Why? To answer this question, one needs to turn back to the conditions for successful integration described in the previous section.

In most cases, the industry manager was not perceived as having an important or relevant voice in the decision. In some companies he was annointed with the blessings of the chief executive, but in many cases, this was not true. In some cases the industry manager appeared to start with this blessing, but was deserted or undercut by top management in confrontations with other functional managers. The members of the organization simply did not believe in the importance of the position or that it was truly supported by top management.

Many industry managers lacked the breadth of experience to demonstrate sufficient expertise to those to be integrated to be convincing. Railroads have not devoted much effort to developing individuals with balanced knowledge, so the ranks of people who could be convincing to both the marketing and operating departments were very thin. So, what often happened was that an individual from one department with limited experience in the other was selected. In most cases, this person came from the commercial area. Almost immediately an attitude of suspicion or intolerance was evident from the operating department. This was often partly justified by the industry manager's lack of broad operating expertise and previous identification with and presumed prejudice for the commercial department.

Also, many of the industry managers were not in a position to see clearly the implications of their decisions and trade-offs, and lacked the information ever to be able to do so. As such, their information and vantage points were not superior to the functional managers, and might have been inferior, since presumably the functional managers at least had the detailed information of their own departments at hand. Even in cases where profit or loss statements were created, there were so many arbitrary cost and revenue allocations in them that the credibility was so low that they provided little management information of any significance to the industry manager. This information was often unconvincing to the department manager, particularly if it suggested that his position should be compromised.

---

[b] One example of the general approach to a market or industry manager proposed to one railroad is described by D. Daryl Wyckoff, *Western Pacific Railroad Company*, (B) (Boston: Harvard Business School, 1974).

In most cases the reward system did not promote cooperation with the industry manager. Whether the industry manager succeeded or failed was often his personal problem; the functional managers were generally judged on more conventional measures of departmental performance.

Also, the industry manager was often in a situation where he was to integrate the actions and inputs of individuals with clearly different power bases and clout. In many situations, those in the operating department had substantially more power than other members of the group, even the integrator himself. When the level of power is so considerably out of balance, the probability of success is low.

Finally, in the cases where the industry manager concept has not succeeded, I would point to a general lack of top management commitment to the project as a major contributor to the failure. This is not to say that top management undermined the organizational innovation. Rather, the problem tended to stem from an unrealistic appraisal of the magnitude of support and reinforcement required to implement such an innovation. The cost (financially and emotionally) of the creation of new management information, redefinition of roles, delegation of authority, and a clear charter of mission were usually far greater than managements were willing to invest. This was particularly true where top management was not fully convinced that the concept was viable or that the return on financial (and emotional) investment would be satisfactory.

The net result of the industry-manager approach to increase integration must be rated as having scored substantially below expectations on most railroads. The extent to which the innovation was successful on other railroads was directly connected to the degree that the conditions for successful integration, listed above, were met.

At present, there are experiments in decentralization and integration being conducted on at least two railroads. So far, there is no clear evidence that the experiments are either a great success or a failure. There may be some reasons for this that are not immediately obvious to the railroads. Besides the fact that some of the conditions for successful integration had to be compromised in an effort to innovate, I believe that the company presently making one of the most sustained efforts at forcing integration into lower levels of the organization may have great difficulty in recognizing (or measuring) evidence of the benefits. Specifically, the more transaction oriented the railroad is, the more evident the benefit of lower level integration will be. The arguments supporting this are discussed in greater detail in chapter 6, but at this point, I would assert that the long-haul railroad, particularly if it is successful in minimizing the number of transactions (yard and local operations) enroute, can cover up a greater magnitude of local problems. I am very concerned that this attempt at increased integration at lower organizational levels will not meet original expectations and management may be discouraged to the point of not aggressively pursuing the discipline and development necessary to see it to the logical conclusion.

Notes

1. Jay W. Lorsch, in an unpublished address before the National Academy of Management, August 1975. Also see Paul R. Lawrence and Jay W. Lorsch, *Organization and Environment* (Boston: Harvard Business School, 1967), p. 3.

2. Alred D. Chandler, Jr., *Strategy and Structure* (Garden City, New York: Doubleday and Company, 1966), chaps. 1-2.

3. Lorsch, National Academy of Management.

4. D. Daryl Wyckoff, *Organizational Formality and Performance in the Motor Carrier Industry* (Lexington, Mass: Lexington Books, D.C. Heath and Company, 1974).

5. Lawrence and Lorsch, *Organization and Environment*, pp. 8-11.

6. Ibid., pp. 11-12.

7. Ibid., p. 12.

8. Paul R. Lawrence and Jay W. Lorsch, "New Management Job: The Integrator," *Harvard Business Review*, November-December 1967, p. 143.

9. Lawrence and Lorsch, *Organization and Environment*, chap. 3.

3

Tasks of Railroad Management

This chapter is a summary description of the activities and tasks of a railroad. It is intended for readers who are not familiar with all the operations of railroads, and it will be of particular value for reference as we turn to the issue of designing an organizational structure to deal with these tasks in the spirit of the contingency organization theory.

I have attempted to minimize the inclusion of any implied organization in these discussions since this is the variable I consider changing. Unfortunately, it is nearly impossible to describe the functions of long-existing enterprises such as railroads without some reference to organization. I recognize the problem but do not believe that some modest unavoidable inclusion of organization here distracts from the overall purpose.

The "railroad functions" described are historical and may be considered by some as too limited a definition of the desirable nature of the railroad business of the future.[a] But my discussion must begin at the point that railroad managers find themselves now, hence, the decision to describe railroading as I have found it today.

Also, there is a problem associated with describing the railroad process. Should the description be that of what I consider a "typical" railroad, or should I point out the many specific variations that might be found? Since the primary purpose of this chapter is to serve as a general background for discussion rather than as a catalog of the state of the art of railroad practices in the United States, I have not attempted to prepare an exhaustive operating handbook. It is intended as a general overview, and I am conscious of the many detailed exceptions to the description. I begin with a brief review of the financial structure of the railroad industry.

I placed the transportation function or "process" early in my description because of my belief that this is the way that most railroaders view its importance. I considered construction and maintenance of way and maintenance of equipment to have a supportive role.

Labor is considered as a separate subject after each of the tasks are described because I believed that it was only at that point in the discussion that the impact of this element could be fully appreciated.

The commercial activities such as selling, pricing, business develop-

---

[a] For a more complete discussion of this issue see: D. Daryl Wyckoff and David H. Maister, *The Owner-Operator: Independent Trucker* (Lexington, Mass.: Lexington Books, D.C. Heath and Company, 1975), pp. 107-25.

Table 3-1
Pro Forma Income Statement of Class I Railroads, 1973

	Percent of Total Revenues
Revenues	
Freight revenue	96.9
Passenger revenue	3.1
Total operating revenue	100.0
Operating Expenses	
Maintenance of way and structures	14.4
Maintenance of equipment	18.3
Transportation	42.6
Other	8.4
Total operating expenses	83.7
Operating income	16.3
Net of taxes, rents, etc.	11.4
Income available for fixed charges	7.4
Less total fixed charges	4.4
Income after fixed charges	3.0
Contingent interest	0.2
Net income	2.8

Source: *Moody's Transportation Manual*, 1974.

ment, and the regulatory and market environment were treated separately, which is consistent with the de facto behavior of many railroaders.

Financial Structure

The railroad industry is composed of 68 Class I, line-haul, operating railroads plus several hundred smaller, operating companies. These Class I railroads, having annual operating revenues exceeding $5 million, represent approximately 99 percent of the traffic carried by railroads and 95 percent of the rail mileage.

Tables 3-1 and 3-2 provide pro forma income and balance sheets for the consolidated Class I railroads. While individual railroads certainly vary from the structures outlined for the industry, these tables provide some insight into how railroads spend their revenues and the types of assets and liabilities that are involved in producing these revenues.

For brief periods, maintenance expenses may be successfully deferred, but transportation expenses are directly related to the operation. Close to 11 percent of total operating revenues are paid out to equipment and facilities rents and fixed charges including interest charges.

Table 3-2
Pro Forma Balance Sheet of Class I Railroads, 1973

	Percent of *Total Assets*	*Percent of Total* *Operating Revenues*
Assets		
Current assets	7.03	20.09
Special fund	0.83	2.37
Investments	9.24	26.40
Transportation property		
(gross)	101.70	290.56
Less: accrued depreciation	27.26	77.88
Net transportation property	74.44	212.68
Misc. physical property	1.96	5.60
(gross)		
Less: accrued depreciation	0.39	1.11
Net properties other than		
transportation	1.57	4.49
Deferred assets	0.77	2.20
Prepayments, etc., other	6.12	17.48
	100.00	285.70
Liabilities		
Current liabilities	9.68	27.66
Long-term debt	32.24	92.11
Deferred liabilities	2.16	6.17
Unadjusted liabilities	7.62	21.77
Total liabilities	51.70	147.71
Stock	12.90	36.85
Corporate surplus	35.40	101.14
Total shareholders equity	48.30	137.99
Total liabilities and		
net worth	100.00	285.70

Long-term debt equals 32.24 percent of the total assets and the ratio of long-term debt to equity is approximately 66.8 percent. While this is not a striking debt to equity ratio, it is still quite substantial. It must be understood that much of this debt is very old. The ratio of fixed charges (interest plus related charges) to debt from tables 3-1 and 3-2 is only 4.8 percent. This reflects a significant proportion of debt from earlier days when interest rates were substantially lower than present levels and railroads were considered good loan risks. If railroads were paying closer to the current prime rate, the small, ordinary income reported would be indirectly eliminated. It should be noted that the ratio of "old debt" to "new

Table 3-3
Comparison of Capital Productivities, 1970

	Class I Railroads (Billions)	Class I Motor Carriers (Billions)	Typical Owner-Operators (Thousands)
Revenues	$ 11.991	$ 6.396	$40 to $80
Ton miles	764.809	85.760	1,500 to 3,000
Investment			
Net working capital	0.630	0.111	$5.0
Investment in road	16.866	-0-	-0-
Investment in equipment	16.684	3.000	34.0
Less accumulated depreciation	(9.013)	(1.458)	(17.0)
Net investment in equipment	7.671	1.542	17.0
Other	0.633	-0-	-0-
Total net investment in operating properties	25.170	1.542	17.0
Total net investment	25.800	1.653	22.0
$ Revenue per $ total net investment	0.46	3.87	2.72
Revenue ton miles per $ total net investment	29.64	51.88	102.27
$ Revenue per $ total original investment in equipment	0.72	2.13	1.76
Revenue ton miles per $ total original investment in equipment	45.84	28.6	66.18
$ Revenue per $ net investment in equipment	1.44	4.15	3.53
Revenue ton miles per $ net investment in equipment	90.70	55.62	132.35

Source: Adapted from D. Daryl Wyckoff and David H. Maister, *The Owner-Operator: Independent Trucker*, (Lexington, Mass.: Lexington Books, D.C. Heath and Company 1975), pp. 121-24.

debt" is changing as old debt is refinanced and additional equipment debt is added.

Table 3-3 compares the capital productivity of railroads and two groups of motor carriers. The primary competitors of the railroads are the owner-operators, who specialize in the truckload market. Table 3-3 clearly illustrates the effect of the owner-operators' aggressive use of their capital investment even if the investment in roadbed is removed from the railroads' investment.

Process

The process of transporting goods by railroad car is complicated by several factors. First, it is obviously uneconomical to operate single cars, so considerable effort is expended to form trains of cars in a prescribed order (all cars for the same destination or area grouped together in "blocks"). This order serves as a means of keeping record of the location and status of cars, and to minimize the shuffling or relocating of the order of cars when they are to be removed from the train. Second, the nature of the technology with its confined guide path restricts easy insertion or removal of cars from a train and limits the flexibility of operation in picking up and delivering cars. If these factors are kept in mind, it is easier to understand the necessity of the seemingly tedious process described in the following sections.

Two separate processes occur simultaneously on a railroad. The first is the physical movement of freight, cars, and trains. The second is the flow of information and transactions.

The physical process begins with a crew, usually an engineer, conductor (foreman), and two helpers, placing a car at a shipper's location (see figure 3-1). After the car is loaded, it is switched by a crew into a receiving track of a yard. The activities of the yard are to process the necessary paperwork concerning the movement of the car and its cargo including entry into the railroad's master record-keeping system, and to place cars into a desired order for creation of trains and other disposition. From the receiving tracks, cars enter the classification yard, a series of parallel tracks connected by switches. Each of the parallel tracks is designated to receive cars for a particular destination or group of destinations. The mixed cars are then sorted by being shoved by a switch engine into the appropriate tracks in the case of "flat switch yards." In the larger, modern "hump yards," cars are moved to the top of an incline and then allowed to roll by gravity through a series of "retarders" (which slow the car to an appropriate speed) and switches that send the car on a path to the appropriate track to couple automatically with other cars at an impact speed of roughly 4 miles per hour.

In addition to cars loaded near a yard, cars may be received by transfer from other railroads or from trains arriving from other parts of the same railroad. In some cases, these may be blocks of cars that were partially classified at other yards, but often they are in random order and require full classification sorting in the same manner as cars received from industry switching.

A train is assembled on a departure track by switching together (doubling over) the strings of classified (sorted) cars. The road locomotive and caboose are then attached. The assigned train crew and car men (mechanical repairmen) make the necessary inspections. Tbe train departs after receipt of the proper authorization. Crews change at agreed locations (commonly called division points), which have been established based on the work required, federal hours of allowable time on duty rules, historical precedents, and labor agreements.

24

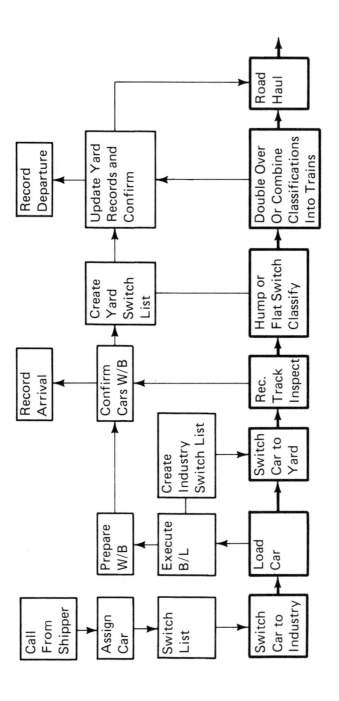

Note: Heavy lines indicate physical movements of cars and freight.
 Light lines indicate information flows.
 W/B = Waybill.

B/L = Bill of Lading.

Figure 3-1. Outbound Yard Operations

At various points in a train's route it may be desirable to drop (set out) or pick up cars at intermediate points. Such setouts are performed in accordance with procedures that state schedules, normal handling of blocks of cars, and disposition of cars at each setout point. Cars to be cut out of the train at a setout station may be classified and switched to industry for unloading and return to service or transferred to another road.

The portion of the train that is to "continue beyond" picks up cars to be received from the setout station. In some cases, these cars may be reclassified into the correct positions in the previously made-up train. However, more frequently, an attempt is made to postpone additional reclassification to the limit of practicality by simply receiving the picked-up cars and inserting them in the train in one block to be sorted later.

The train then progresses through setout points until it reaches its termination.

Figures 3-1 and 3-2 also schematically describe an abbreviated form of the information flow associated with the movement of freight. For the purpose of this description, the illustrative movement is initiated by a request from the shipper to the railroad for a car. The car is assigned and dispatched to the industry location through instructions to a local switch train crew. When the car is loaded and is ready to be released for movement, the shipper issues instructions to the railroad in the form of a bill of lading. The bill of lading is a form of contract specifying the details of routing, shipper and consignee, commodity, and special terms and conditions. This is often telephoned to the railroad and followed by the formally executed document. From this information, switching instructions are developed and a way bill is prepared. The way bill is the document that contains instructions for the movement of the car. It identifies the shipper, receiver, and commodity, as well as routing and any special instructions to be followed. The way bill is matched with receiving reports on arrival of the car in the yard, and it accompanies the car for its entire movement.

At this point, the load is recorded as a shipment for railroad control purposes. This record keeping is generally performed by electronic data processing on most railroads today.

In the yard, each car must be accounted for to insure proper handling. While a number of different systems exist for this purpose, one of the most common is PICL (Perpetual Inventory of Car Location). The PICL system uses a punch card, which is created for each car when it enters the yard. A set of slots or "pigeon holes" representing individual yard tracks serves as a "model" of the yard. As the car moves through the yard, the PICL punch card that represents it is similarly moved from one slot to another. Any one slot contains in order all of the cards representing cars standing on a particular track. These cards become the primary means of locating cars in a yard and are the source of information for creating

26

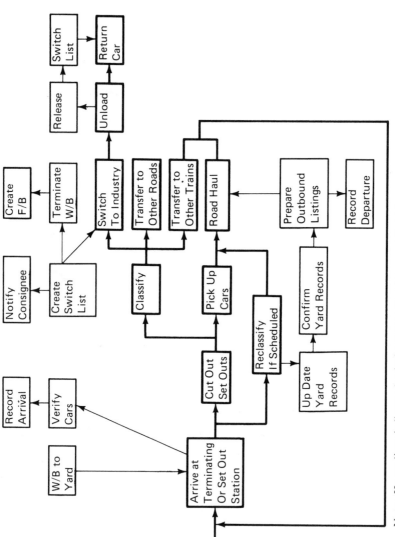

Figure 3-2. Setout or Terminating Yard Operations

Note: Heavy lines indicate physical movements of cars and freight.
Light lines indicate information flows.
W/B = Waybill.
B/L = Bill of Lading.
F/B = Freight Bill.

switch lists and trains consists (contents and order).

The train operating over the road passes under the control of a dispatcher. This control may be exercised in several ways, including:

1. *Centralized Traffic Control (CTC)*: a system by which the movement of trains may be controlled using switches and signals electrically operated by a central dispatcher. The position of trains, switch positions, and signal conditions are indicated on electronic display panels. In many CTC systems, the dispatcher also maintains radio contact with the train crews operating in his area.

2. *Automatic Block System (ABS)*: A system of signals that indicates to trains about to enter a segment of track whether it is already occupied by another train. By creating blocks of relatively short lengths of track, it is possible to move fairly large volumes of traffic in an expeditious manner while maintaining a practice of allowing only one train in a block at a time. This system is usually supplemented by written procedures and special train orders.

3. *Blind or Dark Track*: no signalling with operations depending on a system of written procedures and special train orders.

Upon arrival of a train at a setout station or terminating station, the waybills for the cars that are leaving the train at this point are delivered to the yard office. The cars that have been cut out of the train are verified and records are updated. The setout cars are classified following some form of the confirmation (i.e., PICL) and switch list procedure described before. The waybills for cars being transferred to other trains on the same road or other roads are moved to the appropriate trains. The waybills for cars to be delivered to local industry are terminated. When the waybill is terminated, a freight bill is prepared indicating the origin, destination, routing, commodity information, as well as charges. Some railroads prepare these bills at local stations, but it is now more typical that freight bills are prepared by a central facility.

While the process just described is relatively simple to follow for a single shipment, this is not to depreciate the task of railroad management in controlling the process. A railroad yard may process as few as 100 of such transactions each day, but a large yard will very likely handle as many as 1,500 to 3,000 shipments. The complexity of control appears to increase in a nonlinear fashion as the volume of activity increases.

Figure 3-3 summarizes the amount of time spent by a car in processing through the process described above in a round-trip cycle. Several problems experienced by railroads are illustrated by this figure.

First, the average car spends a considerable portion (23 percent) of the cycle outside the hands of the railroad, as seen in figure 3-3.[1] While there are rules and charges for demurrage to encourage prompt processing of cars by shippers and consignees, careful handling and cleanliness of re-

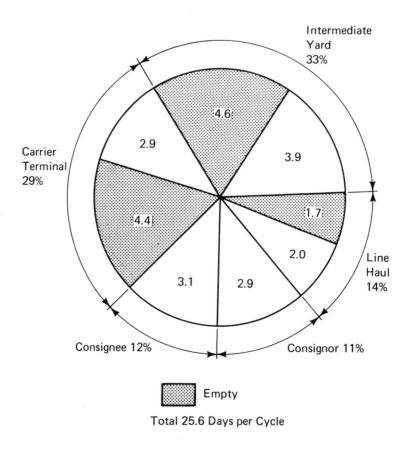

Figure 3-3. Typical Freight Car Cycle (in Days)

Source: *Rail Service in the Midwest and Northeast Region*, vol. 1 (Washington, D.C.: U.S. Department of Transportation, February 1, 1974), p. 9.

leased empty cars, substantial delays in equipment arise directly from these sources that are generally outside the direct control of the railroads. The data in figure 3-3 are based on a study of all car types, all owners, and all commodities. Specific cars, such as covered hoppers, may have an entirely different cycle compared with 65-foot gondolas, for example. Open-top hoppers in coal-unit trains record a relatively low loaded mileage of 50 percent, but deliver vastly more loaded car miles or ton miles each year than other cars in general service.[2]

Second, the average car is in terminals a total of 15.8 days or 62 percent of the time. Even if one were to deduct the average 4.4 days when the car is empty in the carrier's terminal, presuming it is empty and waiting for dispatch, the car is in some terminal activity 11.4 days or 44 percent. These figures are quite striking when compared with the 3.7 or 14 percent of the cycle that is line-haul operations, what many uninformed observers would consider to be the primary activity of railroads. Thus, the majority of the cycle is spent in the tedious local operations of switching and yard processing. A car passing through a classification yard may be expected to incur a delay of one to three days, assuming that the car does not require mechanical repair, all the paper work is in order, and there are no errors or irregularities.

Work rules, full-crew laws, and union-craft designations greatly hamper freedom to operate yards and terminals in the most productive manner. These issues are discussed in greater detail in the section dealing with railroad labor. However, here it is necessary to discuss a significant factor aggravating the yard problem: the practice of operating long trains on some railroads. While this trend has diminished in the past decade on several railroads, much of the industry is still suffering from the effects of this practice.

Largely due to deteriorating labor relations that existed in the industry until the early 1970s, work rules frustrated most attempts to improve labor productivity from technological innovation. Three types of work rules were particularly responsible for this: crew-size and consist rules, basis-of-pay rules, and rules governing the distinction between road and yard work.[3] To attempt to compensate for the restrictive practices of the crew-consist rules, which maintained unnecessary crew members, most railroads employed increasingly more powerful combinations of diesel units to pull trains of increasing length and weight. This decreased the labor cost per freight car mile because the same size of crew was used for the longer train operation. However, these longer trains had several impacts. First, longer trains usually implied less frequent departures, thus a basic reduction in service. Second, longer trains usually required larger yards for the more complex assembly of cars. These larger yards, as discussed earlier, resulted in a more complex operation with greater congestion and tendency for error. As trains became longer, the probability of not making an intended connection increased rapidly. A study conducted by the Department of Civil Engineering at the Massachusetts Institute of Technology concluded that in the large yards studied, "10 to 20 percent missed connections may be usual; 30 percent or more missed connections were not unusual."[4] If the probability of missing a connection at each yard was as high as 30 percent, and if a car passed through an average of six yards on its journey, the probability of missing at least one connection generally meant a delay of at least 12 hours and more typically 24 hours because of the infrequency of departures.

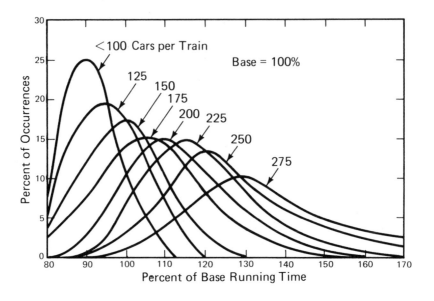

Source: *A Study of the Economics of Short Trains*, Peat, Marwick, Mitchell & Co., June 1974, p. 15.

Figure 3-4. Schedule Reliability as a Function of Train Length

The same M.I.T. study found that yards were generally unsuccessful at accommodating lateness. Once a car was behind its schedule, it was extremely difficult to catch up. The two primary reasons for cars missing their intended outbound connections were outbound cancellation and late arrival of inbound trains. A study conducted by Peat, Marwick, Mitchell & Company concluded that schedule reliability was inversely related to train length.[5] This deterioration in reliability was not only an increase in the mean time, but a spreading of the tails of the distribution, as seen in figure 3-4.

These problems have all added up to deterioration of service reliability and diminished capital productivity. It is difficult to estimate the "economic cost" of unreliable service in a competitive market; however, some crude estimates can be placed on the cost of a delay of cars. For example, Joseph F. Folk and James L. Forester noted, "If the rail industry could average just one more loaded trip per car per year, this would mean an effective fleet reduction of 5 percent. Using annual ownership and maintenance costs of $3,000 per car, this 5 percent reduction translates to an annual saving of about $225 million."[6]

Railroads have expended great effort and investments of capital to improve yard operations. But, delay of cars is minimized and equipment productivity is maximized by avoiding yards whenever possible. This can be partially achieved by preclassification of cars in smaller and less congested yards.

An area of railroad operations that provides an interesting insight to the railroad process and management style is freight car management. For the purposes of this discussion, I concentrate on a comparison of two railroads that are generally considered by other railroaders as being highly sophisticated in the use of computers: Southern Pacific Transportation Company and the Southern Railway System.

Both railroads have defined similar purposes for their freight car management systems. However, there is some indication that Southern Pacific was focusing on optimizing car use and minimizing system empty miles, while the Southern was more concerned with availability of cars at local points, with optimization of use and empty miles for the whole system as secondary. Table 3-4 is a brief summary of my interpretation of the comparison of the systems.

At Southern Pacific Transportation, freight cars and their use are primarily the responsibility of several regional car distributors who make up a central organization. The assignment of freight cars is in the hands of these individuals and the computer system, TOPS (Total Operation Processing System), that was developed by the railroad and IBM Corporation. This system, which is reported to represent an investment of $26 million, is a real-time communication and operation system.

Five kinds of dynamic files provide a basis for distribution and management of cars on the Southern Pacific property. The *car file* contains data on all foreign (from other railroads) cars on line and all Southern Pacific cars, including information about car type, capacity, pool assignment, last interchange receipt and delivery, current location, waybill data, and pending instructions. This file is the key system file for assessing car status and location changes and for car distribution information. The *train file* contains information on all trains in operation on the Southern Pacific at any particular time. The register portion of the file carries data on train schedules, assignments, location, power, and other "departing data" on individual trains. The *yard responsibility file* contains an "image" of each important yard or terminal. It includes information on locomotives on hand, trains to run and to receive, and inventories of cars on hand and in the local vicinity. The *minor area file* covers areas not included in the yard responsibility file, while the *motive power file* contains descriptive data on all Southern Pacific locomotives.

All individual cars recorded in the system are assigned "movement instructions," even if the instructions were to "remain where located." The computer files are storage devices for these instructions. Disposition of empty freight cars is determined by the computer on the basis of the

Table 3-4
Comparison of Computerized Freight Car Management Systems of Two Major Railroads, 1974

Railroad	Southern Pacific Transportation	Southern Railway System
Average number of cars managed	91,000 cars	90,000 cars
Average length of haul	555 miles	313 miles
Miles of track in system	11,477 miles	10,531 miles
Area served	Transcontinental	Southeast
Primary purpose of system	To maintain maximum use of equipment by continuous real-time inventory of specific units by specific locations	Distribution of empty cars to maximize use of equipment at the minimum relocation expense
Primary measures of performance	1. Average number of empty car miles by car type and status per load for each week	1. Ratio of number of empties on hand to daily demand at each location by car type. The target was 2:1.
	2. Average number of empty car miles by car type and status per load for each week	2. Ratio of empty miles to loaded miles by car type
	3. Average number of empty car miles per day	
	4. Car cycle time (from one loading to the next loading)	

Degree of centralization	Two tier system of headquarters group supplemented by six regional car distribution. Offices that provide a high degree of centralized control. Local operations are primarily responsible for updating movement records at car passing or when cars change status. Cars are assigned disposition instructions established by the regional or headquarter car distributors. These assignments are based on a hierarchy of rules.	Maximum decentralization. Belief that local management can best handle car movement problems. The primary management responsibility is left in the hands of local agents. They are to determine the most effective and efficient use of the cars in their area. If surplus cars become available in the area the central car control will then issue orders for relocation following the rule of moving the surplus units to the nearest deficit location.
Local allocation rules	Request instructions from the system.	Use cars if needed locally. Release surplus cars to adjacent areas if requires release the remaining surplus cars to areas designated by central control.
Central and regional control allocation rules	Compare availability and demands for each type of car by location. Route specific cars from surplus areas to deficit areas to minimize the sum of empty car-miles for the system per day. If large quantities of cars were required to move between specific points. Special trains of empty cars that bypass yards are used.	Relocate cars at closest deficit location.

current inventory of cars and their locations, demands, and a set of operating policies stated as computer programs (see table 3-4).

In order for a local agent to determine the disposition of a recently emptied freight car, he merely had to enter the car number on his remote computer terminal. A printout on the cathode ray tube terminal displays instructions as to what to do with the car. In most cases the destination is assigned to the car in the car file and punched in card format for use in the yard. The decision-making process had already occurred, and the agent only had to follow instructions. As a concession to traditional railroad industry practice, a local agent could change a car's disposition if he felt this would provide better service. But a change by a local agent is immediately recorded and labeled as originating from the agent. As a practical matter, the local agents made few such changes.

At Southern Railway, the basic car management function is highly decentralized in the hands of the local agent. As stated by the top management of the railroad, "Local agents can best decide how to use freight cars efficiently and effectively." The railroad has two strategies of car management that they consider to be highly successful at the Southern Railway: "(1) Classes of cars never have absolute orders for movement, and only surplus cars are sent from station areas, and (2) unless there is an overriding reason, cars are sent to fill needs at the nearest available station."

The Southern Railway system is primarily a daily inventory of cars and a record of demands by car type and location. The system provides each location with an accounting of the situation.

Reallocation of cars that are determined to be surplus by a local agent takes place in accordance with a policy called the "flow rule." Under the flow rule, divisions generating surplus empties should send equipment to the closest division with current deficits. In other words, each division takes care of its own needs first, then supplies the residual cars to adjacent deficit divisions, then to deficit divisions beyond. See table 3-4. Of course, all such actions occur only after the local agent had consulted and observed all standing orders from the Association of American Railroads and the Interstate Commerce Commission concerning car rules and instructions on the return of empty foreign equipment to its home railroad.

Obviously, these two systems represent substantial investment in computer technology. Yet, the approaches and philosophies are quite different. I believe that either railroad had the capability and capacity to have elected the opposite system, and the fact that each made its choice the way it did implies a great deal about the operating philosophy of each.

The Southern Pacific TOPS system essentially centralizes control. It stresses the belief that a carefully controlled, centralized group aided by highly consistent rules applied by a computer-based system provides the most rational management system. I do not believe that the Southern Pacific philosophy necessarily implies a demeaning attitude toward the local agent. Rather, it places great faith in "rationalization," systematic application of technology, and optimization of use as a cost minimization strategy.

The Southern Railway system is a highly effective car distribution system in that it is highly consistent with that railroad's overall strategy of localization of decision-making service integrity, while it may lack some of the technical features of the Southern Pacific TOPS system. The Southern Railway choice of systems appears to sacrifice the fine tuning of system optimization in favor of local option and initiative in the hands of local agents.[b]

As seen from the description of the railroad process, this is an industry that has a tremendous number of transactions that occur over a geographically dispersed area. A railroad car moving through its cycle is processed by many different people, each handling a small and possibly seemingly unimportant task in the whole process. The entire process, if not simple, is certainly comprehensible. The complexity primarily comes from the vast number of individual cars and shipments being handled at any time. In this volume of transactions, the subtleties of how each one is handled within the scheme of the system becomes a pattern of performance. When the distance between particular points is substantial, the originating and terminating transactions become a less significant proportion of the whole process. Similarly, if the volume of traffic (or density, to use the railroad terminology) is heavy between two points of significant distance, these are opportunities to avoid the annoying necessities of intermediate transactions to assemble and reassemble economically sized blocks of cars for transportation.

What constitutes effective management of this process? I believe that it is a form of control that trades off the factors of cost, speed, and reliability. The appropriate mixture of these features to achieve most effectively the corporate strategy of a railroad differs in each geographic and commodity market. But it is clear that suboptimization (on efficiency) of any one element of this mix is quite different from effectiveness. *Effectiveness* is defined in most businesses as a "measure of actual output against planned output," where efficiency is a measure that relates the output of a process relative to its input. A manager may be perfectly willing to accept lower efficiency of labor if the process is effective in producing a more appropriate product for the market. The railroads may have become more efficient in producing a service that is increasingly less effective (or ap-

---

[b] Major portions of this discussion are drawn from Michael McCue and W.A. Pinkerton, "Comparative Note on Freight Car Management" (Boston, Mass.: Intercollegiate Case Clearing House, Harvard University, 1974).

propriate) in the market. Efficiency in a system usually implies centralized system management, where effectiveness, particularly in a complex,
dynamic, multimarket situation, implies aggressive and flexible decentralized (in a geographic or product sense) response. How this is best managed depends on demands derived from the inflexibility of the process and
the countervailing demands of flexibility of the market.

Construction and Maintenance of Way and Structures

The functions of construction and maintenance of way and structures are
generally referred to by railroaders as *engineering*. Their purpose is to
provide the facilities on which the railroad operates as a supply or service
activity. This includes initial construction, ongoing maintenance, and improvements or betterments of the physical plant of the railroad. The operations might be generally categorized as civil engineering, maintenance,
and construction.

The amount spent in any particular year for these functions depends
on the stage of development the railroad is in, the extent to which previous investments in betterment or preventative maintenance have been
made, and the extent to which deferred maintenance is practiced.

As discussed in chapter 1, there are basically two ways to organize the
engineering functions: The first uses the separate functional department,
in which all maintenance of way and structures employees report directly
to the chief engineering officer. The second way uses an organization
where the chief engineering officer and his organization are primarily responsible for creating long-term plans and design work, and for setting
specifications and other staff and advisory activities. The actual execution of construction and performance is decentralized geographically under the line organization of the operating organization. No distinction regarding organization is made in the following description and discussion
of the engineering tasks.

The engineering function of the railroad is more or less unique within
the transportation companies in the private sector. For example, the highways used by truck lines are constructed and maintained by state and federal agencies from general tax and specific user-tax revenues. The airlines
make use of the federally operated and maintained airlanes. For historical
reasons, the railroads have traditionally provided their own guide paths.
Some of the very earliest railroads were in fact toll roads that were built
for use by the public. It was not until after the first decade of the operation
of railroads that the purpose shifted to the present concept.

The role of the engineering function and the engineering officers of
railroads quickly shifted as the companies matured. Initially the chief offi-

cer of many railroads was a civil engineer. This was a natural development because of the emphasis on these tasks during that phase. However, within a decade of the completion of the construction of a railroad, the relative importance of the civil engineers had begun to diminish, and a new breed of manager appeared.

Looking at the engineering functions in the order in which they occurred in the construction and operation of the railroad, the preliminary reconnaissance is the first step. This leads to the survey that includes detailed examination of alternate routes, grades, substrata, potential maintainability, wind speeds and directions, snow drift, and potential rock-and-snow slides.

It is hopefully at this stage that there is careful consideration of the potential trade-offs of expenditure of initial investment versus cost of future maintenance and operation. For example, these considerations should include such analysis of grades and curvature versus potential train length, speed, wear, and fuel consumption.

At present, these activities represent a diminished portion of the expenditures of an American railroad. Few railroads are presently constructing main-line track today. The construction function is primarily limited to extensions and new yard facilities, and branch lines and sidings to industry. While there are many variables that influence the cost of construction of track, at present, the cost of a mile of ordinary track constructed on level ground requiring no fills, cuts, or bridges might be estimated to be about $260,000. With average grading, bridge, and land, the cost is about $900,000 per mile.

Once the roadbed has been constructed, the next aspect of the engineering function is maintenance. One problem with the management of the maintenance of way function was summarized by A. Paterson, chief civil engineer of the British Railways. He said, "Railway track engineering is not an exact science." Because of climate, variation of soil conditions, various mixes of traffic carried, and the history of maintenance of a particular track, the practice of maintenance must be a matter of practical experience and engineering judgment.[c]

Unfortunately, this practical experience and engineering judgment has been seriously constrained by limited budgets on financially troubled railroads. Since maintenance is judgmental at some stages, there is a tendency to postpone or defer all but vital repairs when cash is limited. However, while deferment in track renewals can be tolerated for a number of years without apparent effect, there is no escape from the maintenance debt that is built up. "In a relatively short time the essential and unavoid-

---

[c] This is not to say that there are not many important figures in railroading today who are civil engineers by training. However, as a group, these men are among the least parochial civil engineers we met during our field interviews.

able renewals will exceed the renewal capabilities, if not the financial ability to support them."[7]

Because of this condition, most managers responsible for the maintenance of way functions find that substantial portions of their activities are spent in allocating a very small sum of resources to do patchwork repair that has little value except to temporarily restore some level of service on vital lines.

The cost of rehabilitating track to satisfactory condition (not betterment) was recently estimated at $20,500 to $29,000 per mile. Then, after this has been accomplished, it was estimated that a sum of roughly $11,500 per mile for renewals and resurfacing and $2,300 for inspection and routine maintenance would be required over an eight-year cycle.[8]

Closely related, but usually distinguished as a separate function, is the task of betterment or improvement. These are the projects that transcend basic maintenance and include substantial improvement to the road (but fall short of being considered new construction per se). Such betterments are usually treated as capital projects. In several of the railroads where we interviewed, we found that some of the activities designated as betterment projects included installation of new or improved signals, improving grade crossings and bridges, upgrading track to higher standards (such as changing to heavier rail and changing from jointed or bolted rail to welded rail), straightening roadbeds to reduce curvature, and electrification.

As part of all the activities described above, railroads have substantial procurement and subcontracting activities. The purchases of ballast, ties, and rails are in themselves a major activity in the engineering function, whether centralized or decentralized.

Additionally, railroads maintain continuing relationships with private and governmental organizations engaged in planning activities to insure the use of and access to company properties. Also, there are continuous negotiations with private and governmental organizations in matters involving rail-highway crossings.

Finally, the engineering function includes track inspection, testing, and determination of standards for safe operations, including establishing operating speeds and issuing and monitoring slow orders (speed restrictions).

Maintenance of Equipment

The other half of the maintenance function is equipment, the rolling stock of locomotives and cars. As seen in table 3-1 this function, as defined by ICC accounts, which includes depreciation, has recently represented roughly 18 percent on an industry average basis.

Railroad equipment is expensive, but has a long life. For example, a

2,000 horsepower locomotive may cost roughly $350,000; a 3,000 horse-power unit may cost $400,000. Depending on the terrain of a railroad, approximately 1.5 horsepower of locomotive power is required for a ton of train. Basic box cars cost roughly $26,000, but special cars such as large propane cars or covered hopper cars might cost as much as 50 percent more. Under normal maintenance, locomotives may have an economic life span of 20 to 30 years and cars have even longer lives of 30 to 40 years.

Most railroad equipment maintenance operates on an ad hoc and inspect-repair basis. Locomotives are inspected daily. This is not only a company policy, but is also required by the Federal Railroad Administration. Typically locomotives are put in the shop every 30 days, with increased maintenance performed on 90-day, 180-day, 1-year, and 2-year cycles. Most railroads have assigned locomotives to specific "home shops." While routine 30-day inspections are performed at any convenient location, the major shop work is performed at the home shop. This practice is reported to improve identification of the causes of failures and provide better locomotive performance as a result of having to live with problems. One railroad reported that introducing this practice increased locomotive availability by 20 percent.

Most maintenance operations are measured by equipment availability and percentage of equipment in "bad-order" condition. However, equipment maintenance departments are the managers of substantial inventories of supplies and parts necessary to support maintenance and repairs.

The management task of this function is largely complicated by a high degree of uncertainty and ambiguity. As described by one director of equipment maintenance, "There is lots of luck in trouble-shooting a sick locomotive." There have been attempts by some railroads to compare shop times and expense experience to other companies through charges under the AAR inter-railroad billing systems for off-line equipment repair. However, in the railroad industry there are few instances of formal work standards, work measurement systems, and studies of failure frequency (or mean time to failure). Preventive maintenance programs are more the exception than the rule in railroads.

Training in this area is primarily performed on an on-the-job, apprentice-master basis. Some specialized training is provided by equipment suppliers, such as locomotive and airbrake manufacturers.

Labor and the Substitution of Labor-saving Technology

The railroad industry, which spends 51.5 percent of its revenue dollar for labor,[9] has had a long labor relations history that might be characterized by management as militant. In fact, management has had difficulties in maintaining its prerogatives to operate as it saw fit. Labor has continuous-

Table 3-5

Labor Bargaining Units on a Typical Railroad: Kansas City Southern Railway Company, 1975

1. Brotherhood of Railway, Airline, and Steamship Clerks, Freight Handlers, and Express and Station Employees
   A. Clerks' Division
   B. Telegraphers' Division
2. International Brotherhood of Boilermakers, Iron Ship Builders, Blacksmiths, Forgers, and Helpers
3. Brotherhood of Railway Carmen of America
4. American Train Dispatchers Association
5. International Brotherhood of Electrical Workers
6. Brotherhood of Locomotive Engineers
7. International Brotherhood of Firemen, Oilers, Helpers, Roundhouse and Railway Shop Laborers
8. International Association of Machinists and Aerospace Workers
9. Brotherhood of Maintenance of Way Employees
10. American Railway Supervisors Association
11. Sheet Metal Workers International Association
12. Brotherhood of Railroad Signalmen
13. United Transportation Union
    A. Trainmen and switchmen
    B. Firemen and hostlers
    C. Conductors
14. Railroad Yardmasters of America
15. Hotel and Restaurant Employees and Bartenders International Union
16. Brotherhood of Sleeping Car Porters
17. International Brotherhood of Teamsters, Chauffeurs, Warehousemen and Helpers of America

ly battled for several decades to save jobs in a maturing industry and a technological environment that was providing increasing opportunities for the reduction of labor. A craft orientation (compared to an industrywide orientation) seemed to spring naturally from the basic pride (and prejudice) of individual classes of employees, many of which were highly trained, relative to workers in other industries or other railroad workers. As jobs became more threatened, these craft distinctions based on technical training and social structure became barriers for job protection. Thus, the railroad labor movement gave up the potential increased mobility for transfer to new jobs within the railroads as old jobs disappeared with the introduction of new technologies. This evolved into a labor strategy that I characterize as, "We won't let you eliminate us from our jobs, and we would rather fight than switch." The result is an overwhelming maze of unions and individual labor bargaining units. To illustrate the dimensions of this problem, refer to table 3-5, which lists the major bargaining units that one typical railroad management must deal with.

Table 3-6

Decline in Railroad Employment by Major Employment Category on Class I Railroads, 1947-70

Category	1947 (000)	1970 (000)	Percent Decline
Executives, officials, and staff assistants	15	16	8 (increase)
Professional, clerical, and general	224	122	46
Maintenance of way and structures	265	87	67
Maintenance of equipment and stores	370	124	67
Transportation (other than train, engine, and yard)	171	43	75
Transportation (yardmasters, switch tenders, and hostlers)	17	9	45
Transportation (train and engine service)	290	165	45
All employees	1,352	566	58

Source: *The Railroad Retirement System*: Volume I of Staff Papers, August 1972, p. 130.

Labor in the railroad industry has been characterized as hostile and demoralized.[10] To be sure, with each passing decade, the work force of the American railroads has diminished because of changes in markets, mix of freight handled, and technological innovations. These points are clearly illustrated in table 3-6.

However, the operating railroaders I met and interviewed during my research were generally pleased to work for a railroad, had pride in their work, and felt that the actions taken by their labor leaders were justified to save jobs in an unstable industry.

For several decades the railroad industry has bargained with labor from a weakened financial base. When management negotiates from such a position, coupled with a tendency to concentrate on minimizing labor rates to minimize cost, there is a high probability that "management prerogative" will be lost. I see the situation in the automobile industry negotiations to be analogous. The financially strong General Motors has traditionally given up high salaries rather than cave in on work rules and other issues of management prerogative, while financially weaker firms have traded management prerogative for reduced wage rates, which in turn appears to have contributed to further weakening of the companies' positions. I find strong parallels between the trucking industry and General Motors regarding flexibility and management prerogatives, while the railroads and the weaker automobile companies have much in common.

To appreciate the railroad management tasks associated with labor, I turn to the examination of several cases of technological innovations that had potential impact on labor. But first, a brief discussion of work rules in general is in order.

Work rules originally served and continue to serve a number of useful and necessary functions. Railroading is a geographically dispersed operation. It is generally considered to be impractical to have supervisors directing all the operations of a railroad at all times. So standing work rules or orders, in addition to company rules and procedures, serve as standing orders by which the operating employees function. Work rules also serve to protect employees from arbitrary management decisions and actions that may jeopardize their welfare, safety, and economic well-being.[11]

The work rule has largely been the vehicle by which labor has attempted to frustrate management's gain in productivity arising from adoption of technological innovations.

The earliest forms of technology that impacted railroad labor were in track laying and maintenance. Earlier crude construction methods using horse-drawn carts and scrapers and hand placement of ties and rails characterized the basic technology during the construction of most of the major railroads of the United States. Such operations typically used untrained immigrant labor.

Once a section of track was completed, maintenance responsibility was passed to a foreman and a small group of workers. They inspected the track, tightened joints, maintained switches and switch lamps, and made repairs to damaged ties and spikes, using the minimum of labor-saving equipment. Major repairs were made by "extra gangs" of casual laborers, usually hired for the summer months. During layoffs, some higher skilled employees would accept jobs on section gangs as a last resort to keep working. Such low technology and instability and composition in the work force gave labor leaders little to organize around. This group of workers were the most vulnerable to technological displacement. Outside of the railroad industry, new technology for earth moving and civil construction was developing rapidly. As these new construction technologies developed, they were promptly adopted by the railroads. The impact on labor was two-fold: first, most of the innovations were labor-saving devices, which substantially reduced the number of workers required; second, the previous maintenance of way employees generally lacked the skills necessary to operate the new equipment, so the remaining jobs were held by a new class of labor. This served as an early lesson to railroad labor. While the labor movements were ill-prepared to cope with this situation in the early days, the lessons of job protection were learned quickly.[12]

The introduction of the diesel locomotive was perhaps one of the most striking events in terms of railroad labor impact in recent history. The events surrounding its introduction and the workers influenced were substantially different from the previous example. The greatest threat from this innovation was felt by the most powerful and best established of the railroad craft unions. However, as observed by W. Frederick Cottrell, neither management nor the leadership of the affected unions at first perceived how great that impact would be. Management initially saw this as simply being a substitute for steam locomotives and failed to recognize the importance of actively seeking changes in the crew rules. The unions were often more concerned with the division of the jobs between unions rather than protecting jobs. For a while, the engineers protected the jobs of the firemen, but this probably only frustrated the creation of new jobs by expansion of vigorous business.

The diesel electric locomotive could be left unattended and be restarted with relative ease. A diesel locomotive could deliver full horsepower over a wide range of speeds, while the power of steam locomotives tended to be related to the speed at which they operated. One person could easily handle all of the operation of a diesel, thus eliminating the need for the fireman, and to further aggravate the labor displacement, one engineer could remotely operate a string of slave units in the same train that would have required separate individual crews.

Many of the jobs associated with the steam locomotives contracted. For example, there was little need for steam fitters, boiler makers, and water service employees. It became difficult for these workers to protect their status. New tasks appeared in the diesel shops. There was still some need for machinists, but the greater need was for diesel engine mechanics and electricians. There was a low level of conversion of workers between the traditional crafts and the new ones.[13]

The major impact was among the operating employees: engineers, firemen, brakemen, conductors, and switchmen. To understand this, it is necessary to appreciate labor contracts that dictate the payment to crews and the work they may be asked to perform. The typical contract is a complex agreement in force between the management and its work force. It not only covers a variety of operating procedures, but it also defines a standard day's work, and the payments associated therewith, and the variety of extras that an employee may earn for various reasons.

For example, the provisions regulating pay of an engineer had their origin at a time when 100 miles of operation represented a full day of hard work. By the time of World War I, 100 miles of operation itself was interpreted as being the equivalent to a full day of work even it it took less than eight hours. So, it become possible for an engineer to do several full-day equivalents in one work shift of eight hours. Originally refueling and servicing of steam engines were required every 100 miles, so these were established as division points. As these were no longer necessary, new rules had to be created to cover the operation of a locomotive across division limits.

A great number of "arbitrary" allowances for the performance of tasks not originally covered as part of the job were created. In some cases, these became penalties for the introduction of operating conveniences such as pooled cabooses to assigned cabooses. Each time management has attempted to free itself from these arbitraries, the unions have made counterdemands for increased pay, new job classifications, and other consessions.

This led to a new strategy by management. Rather than continue to battle over piecemeal rule changes, management sought the prerogative to restructure all rules. As part of this strategy, a program of public relations was initiated by the railroads to represent the railroad workers, particularly brakemen and firemen, as "featherbedders." This battle continued from 1959 to 1963. In 1962 a special presidential commission recommended that substantial changes in the rules be put into operation. This was protested by the unions and the argument was carried through congressional action to the Supreme Court of the United States, where the recommendations were upheld for a period of two years. About 3,000 firemen were dismissed or "furloughed" with no stated plans for rehiring and the number of switchmen and brakemen was reduced. When two years had passed, great consolidating of positions had occurred on both the labor and management sides. The railroads had given the power to bargain to the National Railway Labor Conference. The operating unions had split into two camps. The engineers, who felt that their efforts to protect others, particularly the firemen, had been costly and of little value to themselves, withdrew from the Railway Labor Executives Association (RLEA). The other four operating unions then combined to form the United Transportation Union (UTU) as part of the RLEA. When the two years legislated by Congress and upheld by the Supreme Court ran out in 1966, the Court ruled that the crew consist or composition was an issue that had to be resolved separately on each railroad. As a result, the UTU struck the carriers individually or in small groups, thus avoiding a national confrontation and rail crisis. This UTU tactic, referred to by railroad management as "whip-sawing," was quite effective, and it was estimated that roughly 95 percent of the jobs were reestablished.

In 1972 agreement between the railroads and the UTU was reached. It was agreed that firemen were not required on most engines. Eventually the issue was resolved, however, it was nearly 35 years after the introduction of the diesel locomotive.

While there are several other issues regarding the railroad work force that are of interest, the following summarizes the situation with the example of the merger issue. As markets, technology, and competitive environments continued to change, the railroads had to adjust their corporate structures and physical systems. This principally occurred through mergers. Today there is great pressure to reduce redundant excess capacity of parallel competing lines and reduce railroad interdependence of connecting lines through mergers. The hoped-for benefit beyond the often-quoted "improved service" is reduced cost. If this reduced cost is truly achieved, it depends heavily on the success of the surviving company to reduce the size of the resulting work force. This again raises the issue of job security. In May 1936 a landmark agreement was made between the railroads and the unions. This agreement recognized the right of management to make technological changes, as long as the seniority system that protected the older workers was maintained. Similarly, the right to reduce employment in response to a decline in demand for railroad service was considered legitimate. However, the agreement forced the merger-seeking management to recognize the job rights of workers of both parties to the merger. This slowed down the merger interests and turned managers toward cost savings by other means.

The Washington Agreement of 1936 provides that when a railroad seeks to merge it must give its employees 90 days' written notice of its intention. Labor is to be consulted on merging the seniority rosters. Also a worker is guaranteed that for five years he shall not be placed in a position worse than he held at the time of the consolidation. He must, however, take a job equal to his job at the time of the consolidation if it is offered, or forfeit his rights. A displaced worker is entitled to claim the wage he made in his previous position even though the job he takes may have a lower pay.

As technological change took place in later years, the Washington Agreement of 1936 served as a model for dealing with dislocation other than that resulting from a merger. However, it has been more typical for workers to be confronted with the choice of taking a lump sum settlement or other arrangements.[14]

There have been some signs of encouragement that the unions have a greater desire to take steps to aid the railroads to survive. By 1972 there were substantial signs that the labor climate was improving. The firemen had essentially been eliminated, except as trainees for engineers. Road crews were being allowed to make setouts and pickups of cars. Road engineers were allowed to tie up (park) locomotives in yards and run through yards without yard crews handling the train. According to Al H. Chesser, president of the UTU, there was a greater recognition of the problems on both sides. The backlog of grievances had been reduced by one-third. As Chesser publicly stated, "The time has come for both sides to stop wasting energy and resources fighting each other and use those energies and resources to our mutual advantage."[15] While the labor situation has improved and the fruits of improved labor productivity have begun to acrue to the industry, there is still a legacy of archaic practices, hostility, and mistrust that complicate the task of railroad management and seriously impair the railroads in being fully competitive with other forms of transportation. There are several examples of how management and labor are experimenting with innovative manning and operations, but at the same time there are more examples of programs that were never implemented.

Here is certainly a major task of railroad management and an important consideration in the design of an effective management organization.

Commercial Functions

I have elected to use the term *commercial* functions because this is what is used by many railroad managers. On most railroads this includes selling, pricing, customer service, market research and development, and advertising (and promotion). It roughly represents the railroads' version of marketing.

Many people have been critical of railroads in this functional area, and some reject the idea that railroads have developed a concept of marketing in the broadest sense. Therefore Levitt states that "the railroads are in trouble today not because the need was filled by others (cars, trucks, airplanes, even telephones), but because it was not filled by the railroads themselves. They let others take customers away from them because they assumed themselves to be in the railroad business rather than in the transportation business."[16] He also points out what he believes is the mistaken "idea of indispensability."

Philip Kotter observed that railroads, like many other companies, progress through a process that leads to the development of a marketing concept. Less critical than Levitt's statements, Kotter believes that these steps include the following:

1. Development of a traffic department to provide customers for existing service
2. Introduction of market research
3. Establishment of an individual to provide direction to the marketing activities
4. Proliferation into specific shipper industry marketing to meet the needs of individual customers better[17]

Kotter differentiates the "sales concept" and "marketing concept." Under the sales concept lies a strong production orientation. "Under the sales concept, the emphasis is that 'we're proud of what we can offer you'." The marketing concept has a strong customer orientation. "The marketing concept says the world keeps changing, the environment is dynamic, new needs arise. No product line [or service] exists forever—it must be revised."[18] While several railroad managers articulate strong statements of marketing concepts for their companies, Kotter seriously questions their effectiveness. He states that whether railroads "are really market-oriented depends on the degree of implementation of the customer viewpoint. Too often, middle management and particularly nonmarketing management do not carry out this philosophy on a day-to-day basis."

Rather than simply relying on Kotter's or Levitt's views of the effectiveness of the railroads in achieving the marketing task, I turned to the judgment of shippers. Typical responses appeared to emphasize that railroads did more selling than marketing.

1. Too much time is devoted to trying to influence traffic from one railroad to another, and not enough time or people to trying to meet their real competition—the motor common carrier.

2. Perhaps the greatest boom will come to rail transport when operations become subservient to sales and traffic.

3. In most instances the railroads do not attempt to accommodate customers' needs. Most frequently, customers are requested and usually required to accommodate to services offered.

4. There seems to be a gap between sales or marketing and operating managements.

5. Historically they (railroads) have devoted sufficient time and effort to selling. The problem appeared to lie in a lack of innovations and communications between sales and operating personnel. Where there has been a greater effort, improved service and more realistic selling have resulted.

6. We have seen no sign of improved marketing and sales methods. After all, when a service industry cannot provide a competitive service, what do they have to sell?[19]

In a survey of shippers, *Modern Railroads* magazine found that 81 percent of the respondents believed that railroads had little or no understanding of marketing.

If railroads concentrate on selling, how well do they accomplish this?

7. Railroad salesmen waste both their company's time and my company's time. They are not well received by the people they call on because they lack training and information.[20]

In the railroads I studied, selling might best be characterized as usually keeping the shippers informed of services, placating service complaints, and attempting to secure attractive rates and services from the railroad for major shippers. This type of selling stems from a model of shipper behavior held by these railroads. Specifically, their actions imply that price is the primary and overpowering selling influence. This may be true in some situations, but there is evidence that this is not universally true for all commodities or situations that the railroads consider to be desirable traffic. The results of shipper surveys of *Railway Age* appear to support this. As seen in table 3-7 reliability receives an impressively high score. In a recent shipper survey conducted by *Modern Railroads*, shippers were asked if they would be willing to pay more for reliable service. Only 46 percent said no, and the magazine felt that this was partially influenced by a fear that a positive response would be an encouragement for price increases without improved service. Also, I suspect that there was a tendency toward a bias since many shippers that had already elected to use more expensive but more reliable service may not be represented in the sample. The same survey asked if poor railroad service had caused a shift to trucks in the respondent's company. In this case, 85 percent answered yes.

Yet, a recent study of responses of a large railroad to sales situations indicated that in the majority of cases studied, the primary action taken by the company to attempt to secure the traffic was price reduction. In most of these cases it was apparent that an improvement in service was at least as viable a selling strategy.[21]

Upon closer examination of why this occurred, I found that this was because the production function was perceived to be less adaptive than price was flexible. This was because of the inflexible nature of the process and the inability of the selling function to achieve a meaningful change in production. This appears to resemble Kotter's "selling concept" rather than "marketing concept."

Regulatory Environment

The railroad industry in the United States is regulated in matters of entry, exits, routes, rates, commodities carried, and finances by the Interstate Commerce Commission (ICC). This regulation certainly influences the nature of the task of railroad management.

The railroads came under regulation by the federal government's ICC in 1887. This commission was originally created to restrain the railroads, most of which had little competition, from monopolistic practices. Also, it was intended to bring a degree of stability to the railroad cartels. The instability of the railroad cartels had led to highly destructive price wars interspersed with price hikes that had been injurious to railroads and shippers.[22]

Also, during this period, it was a common practice for the railroads to price collusively and pool either traffic or profits. This collusion was intended to establish tariffs that would extract monopolistic profits through price discrimination. In many cases, the railroads were able to achieve

Table 3-7
Railroad Shipper Survey Results

1. Which of the following factors is most important in your evaluation of freight service?

Speed	5
On-time delivery	44
Careful handling	4
All equally important	13

2. In your experience, which offers greater reliability of service (i.e., delivery at the promised time)?

Railroads	8
Truckers	50
No answer	8

3. Have you noticed substantial change in the reliability of railroad service in the last five years?

Much better	7
Slightly better	21
No change	18
Worse	15
No answer	5

4. Do you believe railroads are making a genuine effort to improve in this area?

Trying hard	35
Indifferent	25
No answer	6

Source: *Railway Age*, November 27, 1967, p. 47.

this. However, there were frequent disputes that resulted in predatory price cutting.

By the time of the 1887 ICC Act the railroads had indulged themselves in excessive investment of redundant capacity. This came about for two reasons. First, many of the early promoters of the railroads derived their personal fortunes from the profits of track construction. Several of the "robber barons" of this early era had little intention, desire, or ability actually to operate the systems they were constructing. Rather, they built miles of useless lines, awarding sole-source contracts to firms that served as intermediaries to their own personal fortunes. Second, traffic that a railroad originated was not included in the cartel pooling calculation, only that which it received from connections. So there were great incentives for railroads, particularly with substantial redundant mainlines, to build branch lines into what might otherwise be considered marginal revenue areas.

As the proliferation of railroad lines increased, each railroad between major points found that it was less secure in its percentage quota of the traffic pool and the pool was often contracting. When this occurred, the discrepancy between the high marginal cost of carriage and the rate became more striking and the pressures leading toward breaking out of the cartel became greater until a price war broke out. While shippers might have had brief windfall benefits during the rate cutting, they were often short-lived, and soon prices of the surviving members of the industry shot up to recover any losses quickly.

Congress, shippers, and the carriers recognized that some action was required to intercede to achieve greater stability, which led to the 1887 ICC Act. The establishment of the ICC required railroads to publish tariffs and formal notice of increases in fares. The ICC Act restricted price discrimination among shippers of different size and strength. This included the elimination of rebates to large companies and the practice of charging more for a short haul (where a carrier might have a monopoly position) than for a long haul to a further point where rates might be set by competition. This original legislation was amended in 1903 and 1910 to give the ICC powers effectively to administer and enforce its original charter. By the time of World War I, the growth rate of railroads was declining and the ICC appeared to have brought increased stability to the industry, particularly to the railroad cartels, that had become known as "rate bureaus." A procedure for establishing rates had evolved that was generally based on distance and the ratio of value to weight of the commodities carried.

As competition between modes increased and the ability of the railroads to compete diminished, the ICC found that it was necessary to regulate other forms of transportation to protect the integrity of railroad regulation. So truckers and water carriers were partially regulated in 1935 and 1940 respectively. With this action, the ICC increasingly found that it was in the position of having to devise methods for allocating traffic among the modes it regulated. Since it did not have powers to issue quotas directly, it used the power it did have, power over rates. This has led to a general policy of allowing rates of the individual modes to settle at levels that approximately compensate for the difference in quality of service. Operationally, this is defined as letting the rates be established at levels such that some shippers will opt for higher quality service at higher rates while others will accept lower quality service at lower rates. While there are many criticisms of such pricing mechanisms, I believe that the two following are most important. The inherent cost advantages of one mode relative to another mode may have little to do with the service advantages—cost of one mode providing a quality service may or may not have any meaningful relationship or basis of comparison with another mode.

The Interstate Commerce Commission exercises its decision-making in rate cases on the basis of "fully distributed" costs, which includes all of the variable costs attributed directly to the movement under consideration plus a prorated share of the fixed costs. The ICC deems such rates to be "fully compensatory." Many observers believe that such a method of rate comparison works to the disadvantage of the railroads by keeping their rates too high and limiting the opportunity to exercise marginal cost pricing against competitors that have higher proportions of their costs that fall into the variable category. Whether this argument has merit is open to question. While greater rate flexibility and the opportunity to readjust the rates between various commodities would certainly be attractive, it is doubtful that the opportunity to reduce rates in general is hardly what the financially troubled railroads need. Even if lower rates would increase the volume of traffic, there is some evidence that increases have failed to help the railroads when they have occurred. While the Interstate Commerce Commission might be accused of preventing the railroads substantial freedom to reduce rates to compete, the tariff books abound with special "commodity rates" that are little more than authorized rate reductions below the formally established "class rates." Approximately 90 percent of all railroad traffic moves on such rates.[23] Certainly, railroads themselves have raised major objections to the rate reductions proposed by railroads. We believe that the Interstate Commerce Commission has probably been far more guilty of failing to be responsive to requests for rate increases during periods of rapid increases in railroad costs.

Another aspect of regulation that seriously affects the task of railroad management is the issue of abandonment. As was described earlier in this section, there were pressures promoting the overexpansion of branch lines into what were at best only marginal revenue-producing areas. Unlike many businesses, railroads do not have the option of unilaterally withdrawing a poorly performing product or service from the market. Instead, the railroad must endure a long and tedious procedure for abandonment before the Interstate Commerce Commission.

This is a substantial problem. The Federal Railroad Administration recently estimated that the United States railroads incur avoidable losses of approximately $57 million per year from the continued operation of about 21,000 miles of light density lines (originating and terminating fewer than 25 carloads per year per mile of line).[24]

Traditionally, when traffic on a branch line is diminished, the carriers apply for permission to cease operation and abandon the line. Shippers and communities on the lines usually vigorously protest such applications with great success. This usually frustrates the abandonment. The carrier begins a process of attempting to restore profits to the line by deferring maintenance, which ultimately results in higher operating costs and less reliable operations. This sets off a vicious circle of decreasing revenues and traffic and increasing costs, and the healthy portions of the railroads must cross-subsidize the operations. Abandonment has occurred at a rate slightly in excess of 1,000 miles per year. The greatest problem in the process is the absence of explicit procedures and firm criteria for granting an abandonment.

Competitive Market Environment

The railroads have suffered two negative environmental trends: shifting of markets (particularly geographic shifts, as well as shifts in shipment sizes) and the development of aggressive competition.

As stated in an earlier section of this chapter, many observers believe that railroads concentrate too much of their efforts on diverting traffic from other railroads (selective demand within the industry) rather than competing with other modes (selective demand outside the industry) and stimulating primary demand.

The railroads have been painfully aware of the competition they face. However, I believe that they have often misread the nature of the competition and the source. The railroads have attempted to deal with motor carrier competition in several ways. However, these have primarily been negative responses, which have produced few positive results.[25]

Too often, the railroads have directed their competitive reactions at the motor carrier industry in general, and have mistakenly concentrated too much of their energies at the regulated motor common carriers of general commodities. While this group of truckers successfully diverted a tremendous volume of less-than-carload freight from the railroads, it might be more accurate to say that many railroads jettisoned it as an annoying problem that might best be ignored. The regulated motor common carriers of general commodities substantially shifted from their truckload orientation to develop the specialized skills and facilities for pickup and delivery and terminal operations associated with less-than-truckload freight. As this has occurred, these carriers have found that their normal operations are becoming increasingly less competitive with the railroads. They have found that truckload freight can best be used to balance operations to provide marginal income on back-hauls, and is not of primary interest.

The railroad managers have taken comfort in the high average rates per ton mile reported by these carriers. However, such rates are quite irrelevant to railroad competition. In fact, the greater sources of railroad competition from the truck are the private motor carriers (carrying own account traffic) and the owner-operators, who specialize in truckload operations for economic and regulatory reasons.

While the highly visible and organized regular motor common carriers are a convenient adversary, energy spent attempting to frustrate them serves little use. In fact, it is harmful to the railroads because it provides

Table 3-8
Comparison of Owner-Operator and Railroad Costs, 1973-74

	Owner-Operator[a] cents per ton-mile		Railroad cents per ton-mile
1. Fuel	0.41	1. Fuel and power	0.07
Transportation labor[b]	0.61	Other material and supplies	0.14
Depreciation[c]	0.14	Transportation labor	0.48
		Equipment and joint facilities rents and depreciation	0.22
Total	1.16	Total	0.91
2. Maintenance[c]	0.25	2. Maintenance of Equipment[d]	0.22
Tires[c]	0.08	Total	0.22
Total	0.33		
3. Licenses	0.05	3. Maintenance of Way[d]	0.22
Fuel tax	0.12	Total	0.22
Total	0.17		
4. Overhead	0.60	4. Traffic	0.04
Insurance	0.06	Miscellaneous and general	0.09
Total	0.66	Payroll and other	0.15
		Total	0.28
5. Interest	0.07	5. Interest	0.07
Net income after interest[b]	0.04	Net income after interest	0.04
Total	0.11	Total	0.11
Grand total	2.43	Grand total	1.74

Source: D. Daryl Wyckoff and David H. Maister, *The Owner-Operator: Independent Trucker*. (Lexington, Mass.: Lexington Books, D.C. Heath and Company, 1975).

[a] Based on an average-cost owner-operator operating under lease to another carrier. Assumes 150,000 miles per year, no empty miles, and an average pay load of 20 tons.

[b] Assumed a 0.46 cent payment to the driver less approximately 0.04 cents as a 10 percent return on cash invested in equipment and working capital. . . . It is only coincidental that 0.04 cents is the net income after interest for both the owner-operator and railroad figures.

[c] This figure includes some taxes that might be deducted and added to item 3. However, we have considered them to be insignificant and have not made this correction.

[d] Does not include depreciation.

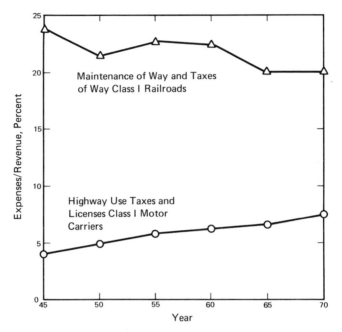

Based on figures from *American Trucking Trends*
and *Yearbook of Railroad Facts* for various years.

Source: D. Daryl Wyckoff and David Maister, *The Owner-Operator: Independent Trucker*,
(Lexington, Mass.: Lexington Books, D. C. Heath and Company, 1975).

Figure 3-5. Comparison of Proportion of Revenue Expended by Class I
Railroads and Motor Carriers for Providing Operating Guide
Paths

railroad managers a false sense of security that far more is being accomplished than actually is. From this point on I will be referring to the truckload competitors in general and concentrate on the owner-operators (generally one-truck fleet operator).

The primary competitive advantages of the truck operator are speed and flexibility. This provides two features simultaneously: First is the obvious benefit of being able to move the shipment more rapidly. However, it also provides the shipper with a substitute for reliability. A fast shipment often carries with it a "halo effect" or sense of reliability it does not fully deserve.

As the railroads have moved to longer trains, more complex yards, and reduced departures, they have tended to reduce speed and reliability of their service, attempting to reduce (labor) costs. On the contrary, the owner-operator reduces his costs by increasing speed. This is primarily derived by the remarkable use of his equipment.

Table 3-8 compares the cost structures of an owner-operator and railroad. We are quick to point out that the owner-operator's costs are 2.43 cents per ton mile compared with 1.74 cents per ton mile. Also, the owner-operator illustrated in the case is a remarkably productive individual at 150,000 miles per year. But, it is clear that owner-operators are within the same order of magnitude of cost with the railroads, and certainly are very competitive with the railroads on higher rated commodities. One of the features of the rail-truck competition that is illustrated in table 3-8 is the role of fuel cost. While fuel costs are a vital ingredient in the picture, it is clear from table 3-8 that they play a less significant role than might first be expected.

Many argue that one of the advantages of the motor carrier is the low cost of highways to truckers compared to the high cost of tracks encountered by railroads. For example, as shown in figure 3-5 the proportion of expenses devoted to maintenance of way and taxes by Class I railroads has declined in recent years, and Class I motor carriers have increased the proportion of revenue paid for highway use taxes and licensing (which are basically devoted to highway construction, development, and maintenance). However, as seen in figure 3-5 the Class I railroads are spending over twice the proportion of their revenues for similar purposes.

Notes

1. *Rail Service in the Midwest and Northeast Region*, vol. 1 (Washington, D.C.: U.S. Department of Transportation, 1974), p. 9.

2. Frank E. Shaffer, "Taking Car Utilization to Task," *Modern Railroads*, July 1975, pp. 56-58.

3. Patrick T. Healy and Alexander L. Morton, *Note on Train Scheduling and Operating Procedures* (Cambridge, Mass.: Harvard Business School, 1974), p. 4.

4. A. Scheffer Lang and Carl D. Martland, *Reliability in Railroad Operations, Studies in Railroad Operations and Economics*, vol. 8 (Cambridge, Mass.: Massachusetts Institute of Technology, 1972), p. 73.

5. Robert H. Leilich, "A Study of the Economics of Short Trains," Peat, Marwick & Mitchell & Company, June 1974, p. 15.

6. Joseph F. Folk and James L. Forrester, "Methods to improve Car Utilization Through Demand Forecasting," *Proceedings of the Transportation Research Forum*, 1975 p. 118.

7. Merwin H. Dick, "Making Bad Track Good: What are the Economics?" *Railway Age*, June 9, 1975, p. 36.

8. Ibid., pp. 36-37. Also see: Lewis M. Phelps, "As Railroads Defer

More Maintenance, Number of Accidents Increases Sharply," *Wall Street Journal*, October 10, 1974; Gail Bronson, "More Disgruntled Shippers Underwrite Routine Railroad Maintenance Inspection," *Wall Street Journal*, October 16, 1974; Bill Paul, "Federal Effort to Reduce Rail Accidents Is a Bust: Many Factors Share the Blame," *Wall Street Journal*, October 21, 1974; Edward T. Myers, "Repair to Meet the Future," *Modern Railroads*, March 1974; Edward T. Myers, "The Cancer of Maintenance-Deferral," *Modern Railroads*, March 1974.

9. *Yearbook of Railroad Facts, 1972 Edition* (Washington, D.C.: Association of American Railroads, 1972), p. 11.

10. Al H. Chesser, "To Our Mutual Advantage," *Handling and Shipping* (President's Issue), 1972, p. 81.

11. John R. Meyer and A.L. Morton, *Improving Railroad Productivity: Final Report of the Task Force of Railroad Productivity* (Washington, D.C.: National Commission on Productivity and the Council of Economic Advisors, 1973), pp. 214-22.

12. W. Frederick Cottrell, *Technological Change and Labor in the Railroad Industry* (Lexington, Mass.: Lexington Books, D.C. Heath and Company, 1970), pp. 120-21.

13. Ibid., pp. 129-30.

14. Ibid., pp. 145-47.

15. Chesser, "Mutual Advantage," p. 84.

16. Theodore Levitt, *Innovation in Marketing* (New York: McGraw-Hill Book Company, Inc., 1962), pp. 39-40 and 71-73.

17. Nancy Ford, "Do We Really Understand Marketing?" *Modern Railroads*, August 1972, p. 26.

18. Ibid., p. 27.

19. Nancy Ford, "The Customer Speaks," *Modern Railroads*, November 1974, p. 75.

20. Ibid., p. 75.

21. D. Daryl Wyckoff and David H. Maister, *The Owner-Operator: Independent Trucker* (Lexington, Mass.: Lexington .. Books, D.C. Heath and Company, 1975), pp. 136-37.

22. Meyer and Morton, *Improving Railroad Productivity*, pp. 187-94.

23. Louis Schneider, "Note on Transportation Rates" (Boston, Mass.: Intercollegiate Case Clearing House, Harvard University, 1964), p. 3.

24. Meyer and Morton, *Improving Railroad Productivity*, p. 160-61.

25. Wyckoff and Maister, *The Owner-Operator: Independent Trucker*, pp. 110-25.

4

Nineteenth-century Origins of Present Railroad Organizations

To understand present railroad organizations fully, one must turn to the developments of the nineteenth century, when the railroads were emerging. This was a vigorous and innovative period in the life of the railroad industry, as shown in this chapter. As the management tasks of the emerging companies shifted from the financial promotion and construction to the operating and administrative phases, substantial creativity in organizational design occurred.

In many respects, the railroads were pioneers in designing organization structures to manage large enterprises. Other than some background from the experiences of the church and government, the military was the primary source of guidance for the development of such organizations. However, even this experience could not be applied directly to the business situations. So, not being able to rely on a body of developed organizational theory, conventional wisdom, or tradition, the early railroaders innovated. Since they were designing organizations to cope with specific situations, rather than universal solutions, they were actually applying the contingency organization theory (that was not to be articulated until nearly a century later).

I describe the British and American experiences in detail. The British experience should be included for two reasons: First, the British railways predate the early United States railways by approximately one decade; thus British managers had to cope with administration of railroads at an earlier stage. While there was not a great transfer of the British administrative experience to America, some communication did occur. This certainly took place when the early American railroad developers were purchasing their first locomotives and rolling stock in England. Second, the early British solutions to designing railroad management structures took a direction that was different from the American solution, although many of the problems and tasks were nearly the same at the early stage. Since one purpose of this book is to examine alternate forms of railroad organization and management style, it is appropriate to include some analysis of this foreign experience. The British approach to railroad management of course transcended the boundaries of the United Kingdom and had a major impact on the organization of the several important railroads of the British colonies and dominions.

In both cases, the railroad industries originally viewed their primary task as management of large-scale construction projects. Also, both the British and American railroad industries initially appeared to be unaware of the great differences in management tasks that occurred with the shift from construction to operations. In most situations, the costs associated with construction far exceeded the original expectations, and the operating managers generally began operating business with companies that were close to financial ruin.

In Britain the railroads were initially created to compete directly with an established inland waterway system, while the American railroads more typically did not have such well established intermodal competition.

As seen in the following historical descriptions, the management organizations of the two industries were influenced by their competitive situations. The British found selling or traffic solicitation and other commercial activities to be quite vital immediately and recognized this in the creation of the position of the goods manager. The earliest American railroad organizations did recognize a commercial role, but it was that of agent, or one who conducted the commercial transactions on a local basis. As the American railroads developed, they found they were largely monopolists in some areas, which required little commercial or highly competitve activity with other railroads. This competition, when not reduced by the promotion of cartels, most typically took the form of price warfare. Under such circumstances the role of the commercial activity was little more than that of communicating the rates to the shipping public. This was clearly a secondary role compared to the massive task of handling freight and operating trains. As the American industry settled into a pattern of rationalization and concentration and regulation, there was limited intermodal competition to justify increasing the status of the commercial function. Also, the end of the nineteenth century was well before the articulation and popularity of the "marketing concept."

So in most respects the railroad management organizations of the nineteenth century were quite appropriate for the tasks, and railroad situation of that period. The main tasks were associated with operating the railroad and the primary organizational design issue appeared to be the degree of decentralization of operating management, given that telegraph and office car travel were the primary tools of communications. The secondary issue was to determine the appropriate degree of integration of train operations and maintenance of the productive facilities. Commercial activities were of far less consequence and appropriately were not to distract attention from these other more important management tasks.

This, together with other early behavior of managers, established many of the attitudes in the industry that are still latent today after conditions have changed.

British Experience

Before describing my interpretation of the early British experience, I should note three points that influenced thinking in early nineteenth century Britain.

At the time of the construction of the first railroads in England, a well-organized, rather complete canal system was in operation. These canal organizations were developed to provide right-of-way facilities on a toll basis to their users who operated their own barges for hire or to carry their own goods. Thus, the canal companies were primarily providers of facilities and were not engaged in carrier services. When the first railways were constructed, they were operated in this same manner, that is, as toll-roads.[1] Although separation of track ownership and operation was found to be impractical, even as late as 1845 there was some evidence of tolling operations on railroads in Britain. Of course, this led the early British railroads to concentrate on problems of construction, maintenance, and toll collecting rather than operation of trains. Drawing on the experience of the canal companies, the early railways were divided into geographical districts to perform these limited functions. In that there was little systematic interaction between the districts in these activities, the free-standing and separate districts proved to be a satisfactory structure at this stage.[2]

The second point to note was the belief of early railroads in permanence of the steel rails.[3] It was assumed that the rails, once properly put into place, would last at least a century. Thus, the role of maintenance of way was minimized in early organizations. (It might be noted that it was not until the second and third decades of railroad operation that the concept of depreciation, a previously unknown accounting concept, was introduced in railroads to provide a noncash expense to be reserved for track replacement.)

Third, England of this period was full of military officers who were returning from duty in the Empire, particularly the Navy and the East India Company Army.[4] These officers represented a substantial pool of experienced leaders and administrators of large enterprises who were anxious to return to England to make their mark in the booming Industrial Revolution.

Construction costs of the railroads greatly exceeded the original estimates of the promoters and builders. This not only presented problems during the construction phase, but proved to be a lingering problem for those who attempted to operate them as commercial ventures thereafter. While the engineers and builders of the railways were elevated to positions of prominence in public opinion at one point of the "railway mania," they were severely criticized by the late 1830s. The engineers became the targets of abuse by pamphleteers in such papers as *An Exposure of the Costly Fallacies of Railroad Engineering* (1837)[5] and *Railways: Their Uses and Management* (1842).[6]

One critic, concerned with extravagance in the use of labor and materials commented that the engineers had proved their "utter incapacity" for "not only economical construction, but economical and thus profitable working." He warned that the railway directors' ignorance of "principles or details of the works"[7] placed them completely in the power of these engineers. Not only were the engineers found to fall short in ability to manage operations, they were accused of being incompetent to manage the commercial or sales activities of the railroads, which were vital because of the railroads' competition with the canals. As long as the railroads remained small it was practical for the directors to exercise reasonable control over the engineers. However, the first railway directors have been described as "amateurs, rarely devoting sufficient time to their duties." Often directors were selected for "political, commercial, or even social reasons," and a directorship was considered a part-time activity. This had led to a loss of control of the enterprise. In the early 1830s a concept of management that separated the role of director and manager began to evolve. The new managers, who were seldom the engineers and who had been engaged in the construction of the railroad, were given new responsibilities. Specifically, as exemplified in a memorandum of the chairman of the London and Birmingham Railway in 1836, each department should be directed by a responsible officer. He was to manage the "details of the business" and make periodic reports to a committee of management or the board of directors. To handle the coordination of the reports to the board, a general manager and secretary were appointed. While the division of responsibilities between these offices was ill-defined, the secretary appears to have concentrated on financial matters. There was no separation of the operating and commercial functions, and they were both the interest of the general manager.[8]

As a leading example of the British experience, I chose the development of the London and North Western Railway, and its innovative and controversal managing director, Mark Huish. With the reduced influence of engineers, men with military experience became attractive candidates for railway management. Captain Mark Huish, described as "last of the East India Company's Army," was one such individual. His early railway management experience was as secretary of the very small Glasgow Paisley and Greenock Railway from 1837 through 1841 and secretary and general manager of the Grand Junction Railway from 1841 through 1846. At that time, the Grand Junction, London and Birmingham, and Manchester and Birmingham railways were merged to from the London and North

Western Railway. It was this merger that put Huish and his concept of management and organization to the test.

By 1846 the concept of making individuals responsible for the activities of subportions of the railway was generally accepted. Also, the board of directors had divided itself into smaller groups to handle specialized matters such as operations, finance, and construction. At this stage, there was little evidence of a structure to the various functions and responsible members of the company. The reports were informal and the process might be characterized more as direction or dictation of the subordinates by Huish rather than delegation of authority and management in the modern sense. Huish, like many other managers who had come from military backgrounds, exercised dictatorial and harsh discipline.

In 1848 and 1850 bills were passed in Parliament to restrict managerial freedom and enforce accounting and reporting practices for the protection of investors.[9] Huish, who strongly believed in formalized reporting seized this opportunity to codify and clarify the practices reporting of the London and North Western Railway (L and NW). He created distinctions between capital and revenue accounts, and depreciation accounts to deal better with the development of the long-run costs of operation. These concepts were not only used for public reporting, but were also used as the important step to formalize the reports of the departments to Huish.

Initially after the 1846 merger, the organization was divided into three divisions that roughly approximated the three railroads that were merged to form the L and NW. This organization tended to lead division managers to suboptimize the operating performance of the system to the advantage of the individual divisions. A series of committees began to be formed in each division, but it was not until 1848 that Huish initiated a structured organization, as shown in figure 4-1, to promote examination of activities involving the whole of the company's operations.[10] These included audit, general finance, general locomotive and merchandise purchase, construction, and real estate. This super structure existed above the regional committees with responsibility for road, locomotive operations, and dispatching on each division. In addition a number of ad hoc committees were created to deal with special problems. While this produced a rather fluid and intermittent form of management, it was a major step toward regularized relationships between "differentiated" departments. However, Huish was the vital ingredient in holding the loose coalition of committees together. He appears to have been omnipresent in the recorded minutes of most committees, and he appears to have performed the role of integration. The structure might have been more functional had Huish been more willing to delegate matters. The overall performance of the company appears not to have suffered because of Huish's failing in

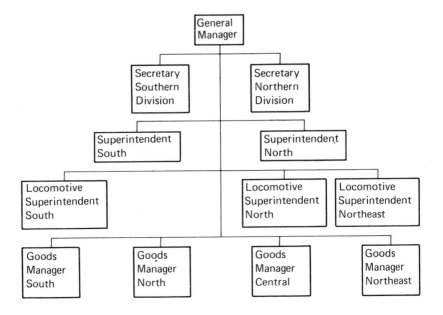

Figure 4-1. Organization Structure of the London and North Western Railway, 1848

this regard, only because of his great personal energy, detailed knowledge of all aspects of operation, and ability to make rapid decisions. However, the L and NW was to have a major change occur in its organization in 1851.

In 1851 Huish essentially weakened the geographic (regional) divisions and strengthened the functional committees and departments. My interpretation of the resulting organization is shown in figure 4-2.[11] Some use of ad hoc committees continued to resolve special problems or handle negotiations or conduct service experiments. Central control of functional groups that in turn controlled regional activities had evolved. This centralization was intended to increase control and reduce costs while improving service during a period of intense competition. The competition had arisen as a result of construction of parallel lines that diluted markets during the railway mania.

As intermodal competition diminished and the competition between railroads reduced with rationalization of the parallel capacity, the commercial functions became increasingly more isolated and reduced.

The development of the L and NW organization provides an interesting case for examining the evolution of a management structure, the role of information, and the role of an individual.

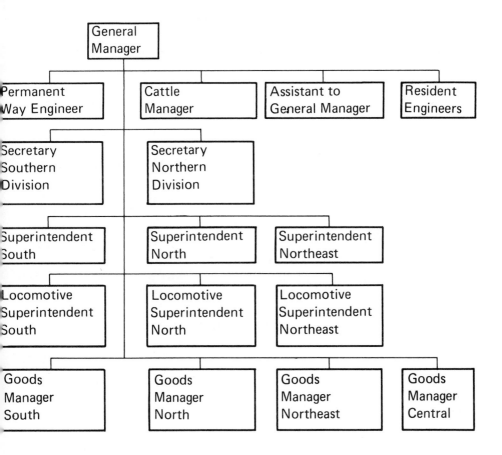

Figure 4-2. Organization of the London and North Western Railway, 1851

I interpret the 1841 organization as an attempt by Huish to continue personally to exercise control and direction of the activities of the L and NW. As an informal and intuitive manager, he attempted to centralize activities rather than create (or permit) a decentralized organization. This pattern of behavior of informal managers under pressure has been seen in the motor carrier industry as well.[12] A second way for an informal manager to maintain control of a growing business enterprise that he wishes to control centrally is to shift to a more manageable mix of activities. For example, he might shift to operations that minimize transactions. In the case of railroads, this might mean shifting from general merchandise or parcels shipments (less-than-carload traffic, in American terminology) to shipments of bulk commodities. With attention to cost control, centralization of decision making which probably implies a loss of vigorous local service and selling, bulk operations are an attractive form of traffic. In this case, the strategy appears to have stemmed from the structure, which in turn was derived from the personality of Huish attempting to cope with the railroad technology. This is clearly the reverse of contingency organization theory in the more conventional sense. This pattern of organization eventually failed for a lack of communication in the nineteenth century, even in relatively compact Britain.

Huish, as a well-respected innovator of British railway management, left a legacy of conventional wisdom regarding railway organization and arrogant management behavior that was to haunt British railroads for years. While the steps he took were suitable for him, his practices were adopted by generations of other British managers and applied as a precedent in less appropriate situations. He certainly instituted reporting and managerial accounting concepts that would significantly contribute to more systematic and sophisticated decision making. However, this was all based on the premise that decisions were to be made at the center. Huish's relative success appears to have arrested development of an alternative management style and structure of vigorous decentralized management.

The American experience, perhaps because of the greater distances in geography and competitive environment, took a different direction at this early stage.

American Experience

The task of managing railroads in the first half of the nineteenth century must be placed in context. They were much larger and more complex (in terms of financial, geographical, and operational scale) than previous private enterprises; thus railroad managers had few historical precedents to turn to in developing organizations to cope with their unique problems. As noted by the business historian Alfred D. Chandler, textile factories were the largest manufacturing concerns in the mid-nineteenth century.[13] While some of these mills had cost as much as a half million dollars, only 41 American plants had capitalization in excess of $250,000 in 1850. Other transportation enterprises (particularly the canals) were significant, with the monumental 360-mile-long Erie Canal costing slightly over $7 million to complete in 1825.

In contrast, several railroads exceeded this level of investment at even the earliest stages of their devlopment. For example, the Western Railroad of Massachusetts was capitalized to $10 million by 1854 and the New York Central reflected an investment of $30 million as early as 1860.

While these early railroad investments appear massive in comparison to other ventures of their day, they would seem modest a few years later when the New York Central approached $150 million by 1883 and the Pennsylvania Railroad represented capital of nearly $400 million by 1873.

The challenge of managing the geographical dispersion and complexity of a coordinated operation was as great as the financial challenge. Even the largest manufacturing firms of the period confined their operations to one or two locations, which made it possible for managers to view their entire operation and to confer conveniently with any employee in a matter of an hour or two, if not minutes. This obviously reduces the problem of coordination, control, and direction.

Canal managers, while managing geographically dispersed operations, had relatively narrowly defined tasks of directing routine maintenance and collecting tolls from the privately operated canal boats over a limited portion of the total mileage of the canal system. Thus, they were not responsible for coordination, operation, nor maintenance of vehicles.

Of course, railroad managers had the tasks of construction and maintenance of way, as well as one of the most complex tasks of operation and coordination of technologically advanced machinery ever seen to that point in history. By the mid-nineteenth century, several railroads were operating hundreds of locomotives and cars over systems covering hundreds of miles each.

It is in this setting that we find the Western Railroad of Massachusetts breaking new ground in business administration. The tracks of the 160-mile railroad were completed by 1841. Almost immediately a series of fatal collisions occurred arising from the company's desire to maximize the productivity of the line. Before this date, shorter lines had followed the practice of limiting the operations to that of one train on the line at any one time. This became impractical as the lengths of the lines were increased. The October 5, 1841 head-on collision of two passenger trains on the single-track, unsignaled mountain system brought about a storm of protest. The Massachusetts legislature initiated an investigation into the cause of the accident that killed a conductor and a passenger and injured seventeen others. It was determined that the Western Railroad had been lax in discipline, coordination and planning of operations, and transmission of detailed orders to train crews. This led the board of directors to appoint a special task force of prominent directors to create a structure and set of general rules to deal with the problems of this relatively large and complex enterprise. In the deliberations of these four men, Elias Haskey Derby, Nathan Carruth, Abraham Lowe, and George Whistler (the Western Railroad's chief engineer), was the genesis of the concepts of railroad organization.[14]

This experiment in creating a management structure serves as a useful background to examine future organizational innovations and develop-

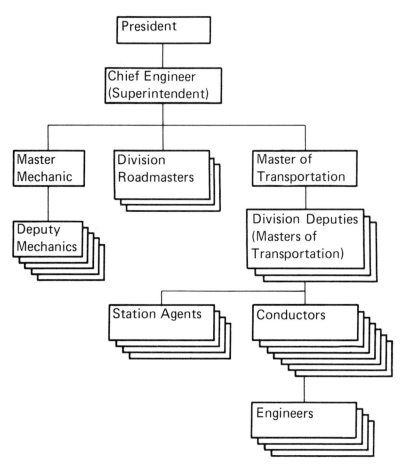

Figure 4-3. Organization of the Western Railroad of Massachusetts, 1841

ments. (See figure 4-3.) The primary objective of the organization was to promote safety. However, considerably more was accomplished in establishing definite formal responsibility for the individual functions of the total enterprise.

The operating organization, under the chief engineer (later to become the superintendent) was divided into three functions that dealt with mechanical repair of operators' equipment, maintenance of way, and operations of trains and stations. This initial division of activity was primarily functional at the top and was then subdivided along geographical lines at lower levels. For example, in one location there might be several different groups of Western Railroad employees reporting through their individual division deputies to functional masters in the company headquarters in

Springfield, Massachusetts. The division roadmasters did not have a formal master, probably because the chief engineer had historically performed that function, and perhaps it was generally accepted that this relatively well-established task could be decentralized. Clearly, it was believed that decentralized train coordination ultimately had to be integrated at one point.

It was at this point that another significant innovation occurred: the fixed-time schedule. The carefully designed and faithfully followed time schedule, together with detailed instructions to be followed to warn other trains on the system in case of breakdown or delay were vital steps in the minimization of future accidents. It also led to several generations of railroad employees who worshipped schedules and had something approaching a fetish for highly accurate watches tested and maintained by railroad certified and approved jewelers.

Shift from the Construction Phase

The more significant early examples of the shift from the construction phase of railroad management were the cases of the Baltimore and Ohio, Erie and New York, Pennsylvania and New York Central railroads. Each of these companies made important nineteenth century contributions to the development of the concept of railroad management in America. The Baltimore and Ohio established the concept of functional specialization, the Erie and New York further developed the organizational concept, but more importantly pioneered the development of management information. The Pennsylvania broke the ground in the development of the concept of line-staff relationships. All four of these railroads established organizations by conscious design.

The first case for examination is the Baltimore and Ohio Railroad (B&O). In 1846, as the major portions of the B&O were being completed, Chief Engineer Benjamin H. Latrobe and President Louis McLane agreed to develop a new system of management appropriate for the scale of operations of the geographically dispersed company.

Prior to 1846 the railroad, under the chief engineer, was divided into several divisions for the purpose of constructing the system. Each division was supervised by an assistant chief engineer who was responsible for all aspects of the construction and completion of his segment of the railroad following the organizational pattern established earlier by the canals.

In 1847 McLane and Latrobe established the objectives for the new B&O organization. In general these objectives would put supervision of all departments geographically closer to their activities. Division of labor was intended to "insure a proper adaptation and daily application of the supervisory power to the objects under its immediate charge." Another objective was to effect strict responsibility, particularly in matters concerning the collection and disbursement of money, purchase of materials, and control of expenditure for repair of way and equipment. It was clearly stated that this new system of management was intended for the ongoing operation of the B&O rather than construction.

The new organization, as seen in figure 4-4, was divided into two major differentiated functions: first, the working of the road'; and second, the collection and disbursement of revenue. These two departments, although equal as regards subordination, had their business so much blended that they were mutually dependent on each other in almost all their transactions.

The financial and control function were under the direction of the treasurer. He was responsible for preparation of financial reports to the president and board and external financing, issuing of securities, and distribution of dividends. He was responsible for the direction of the internal transactions conducted by the secretary (who became known as the controller) and collection of data for the chief clerk's "daily comparisons of the work done by the road and its earnings with the monies received therefore."

The operating function was under the direction of the general superintendent. Reporting to him were the masters of road, machiners, and transportation. The master of the road was responsible for maintenance of the road, buildings, depot structures, water stations, and other fixtures. This was accomplished through local supervisors; foremen; and bridge, water station, and switch operators. The master of machinery maintained locomotives and cars, and buildings in which they were sheltered (i.e., round houses and shops).

The master of transportation was responsible for the working of trains and stations. He directed the work of engineers, firemen, and conductors on trains, station agents and their clerks, porters, laborers, weight masters, watchmen, and car regulators. While the master of transportation was to check reports and records of his subordinates, he also was to make weekly trips over the entire road. It was this need for travel for the purposes of communication generally conducted in the business that seriously limited the geographical span of control exercised by superintendents.[15]

The development of the New York and Erie organization might be viewed as a refinement on the Baltimore and Ohio structure. The objectives of the Erie directors in creating a management structure were to define smaller operating units and assign operating cost responsibility (or accountability) on a system of greater geographic dispersion. It had been ob-

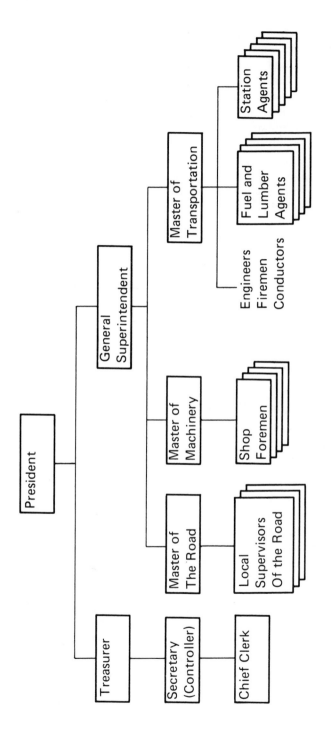

Figure 4-4. Organization of the Baltimore and Ohio Railroad, 1847

served by the directors that the Erie's costs per mile were clearly higher than those of shorter lines. One step in this direction was to break the system into operating units of manageable size that more closely resembled the well-operated smaller roads in 1853. In 1854 Daniel C. McCallum was promoted from the superintendent of one of the new small divisions to general superintendent. As an engineer and inventor, he approached the design of management structure in a highly systematic way. He struggled with the inconsistency of theory, that suggested economy of scale (of longer railroads), and the practical matter that the return to scale was not being realized on the Erie. He observed that even the most imperfect system and superintendent could successfully manage a road of 50 miles. The manager could be fully aware of nearly everything that occurred, know every employee, and personally direct all actions comparatively successfully. While McCallum agreed with the concept of dividing the longer railroad into smaller and more manageable divisions, he also believed that the scale of these regional divisions could be expanded greatly by the use of rapidly communicated, frequent, and detailed management information.

The Erie organization generally resembled the earlier Baltimore and Ohio structure, as may be seen in figure 4-5. However, several new categories of officer were seen to emerge outside the field operating organization. These were:

1. General freight agent
2. General ticket (passenger) agent
3. General wood agent
4. Superintendent of telegraph
5. Foreman of bridge repair

The general freight agent was responsible for creating, publishing, and regulating general prices for the transportation of freight, negotiation of special long-term or volume agreements for freight transportation with companies and individuals. He was also responsible for investigation of claims for damage and loss of freight or baggage and to recommend the form of settlement to be made by the general superintendent. There was little to suggest that he could create new services or modify the offering of the railroad.

The general ticket agent performed similar duties for passengers, as well as supervision of all matters connected with the sale of tickets.

The Erie organization, like the previous Western Railroad of Massachusetts and Baltimore and Ohio, stressed functional differentiation rather than integration at the divisional level. In the words of McCallum, "All subordinates should be accountable to, and be directed by, their immediate superiors only." In this scheme of organization, all superior relation-

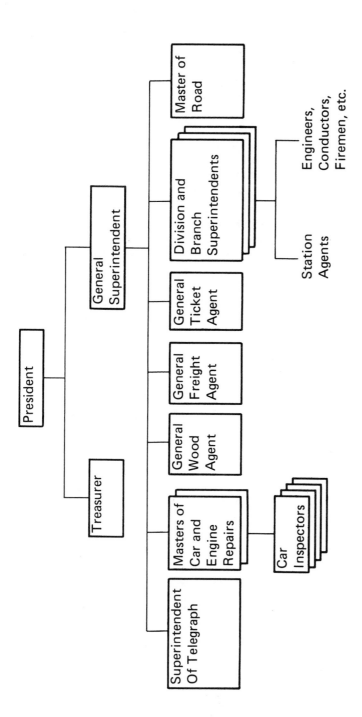

Figure 4-5. Organization of the Erie and New York Railroad, 1854

ships were functionally differentiated except for integration at the very top of the organization.

It must be remembered that I am discussing the period when telegraph was first becoming a practical innovation. In 1844 Samuel Morse demonstrated to the U.S. Supreme Court that it was possible to send a message from Washington to Baltimore with the famous transmission of the words, "What hath God wrought." By 1851 there were approximately 50 telegraph companies in the United States. Initially the telegraph offered the opportunity to provide a means of transmitting information on the status of trains in the system. It was McCallum who saw the great potential for transmitting management information. As an enthusiastic supporter of the telegraphic process, McCallum seized upon this opportunity. In 1854 he proposed that an additional telegraphic system (beyond the signalling system) be installed in the Delaware Division (extending from Port Jervis

Table 4-1
Management Reports of the New York and Erie Railroad, 1854

Passenger Conductors' Reports (Daily)

    Designating numbers of cars used on trains
    Designating numbers of locomotives used on trains
    Names of persons employed on trains
    Arrival and departure times of trains at all stations
    Details of delays or other aspects of trains

Freight Conductors' Reports (Daily)

    Same as passenger conductors, plus description of contents; origin and destination; and waybills for each car

Station Agents' Reports (Daily)

    Times of arrival and departure of each train
    Name of conductor and engine number of each train
    Cars and tonnage added or left at each station
    Record of overs, shorts, or damaged freight
    Delays and causes
    Summary of baggage handled

Division Superintendents' Reports (Monthly)

    Number of (train or car?) miles operated
    Engineer and fireman expenses
    Cost of oil, waste, and tallow for each engine in the division

Master of Engine Repairs' Reports (Monthly)

    Amount expended on each engine for repairs

General Wood Agent Reports (Monthly)

    Amount of wood (cords and expense) for each engine

Station to Susquehanna, Pa., a distance of 104 miles) to provide through messages as a pilot program to be adopted for the entire system.

This system was intended to provide data for management information to determine the potential profitability of the movement of every train. As summarized by McCallum, "By the introduction of a system of reports, and the use of telegraph, much has been accomplished in obtaining these and other desirable results; and when the telegraphic system shall be fully matured and carried out, I have the best of reasons for believing that its efficacy will justify the most sanguine expectations."

The desirable results that he hoped to achieve were:

1. The most effective use of motive power
2. The regulation and reduction of speed to the lowest standard consistent with the exigencies of business
3. The means of controlling the movement of rolling stock, that the greatest amount of service may be derived therefrom
4. The reduction of dead weight (weight of cars), and a corresponding increase of useful load (weight of freight) hauled
5. The reduction of friction, by which the cost of repairs of rolling stock is diminished, and the facilities for economical transportation are proportionately increased.

To achieve this, McCallum created a large number of daily and monthly reports that pinpointed and highlighted the activities of every division and functional group. These reports, summarized in table 4-1, were in addition to the hourly reports on the operations of individual trains that were transmitted by telegraph to the general superintendent's office and recorded in tabular form for every division of the road.

McCallum used the information from the reports listed in table 4-1 to deduce the following information:

Speed of the train between stations

Average load carried in each car

Tonnage of useful load carried

Tonnage of cars in which it (the load) was transported

Tonnage of empty returned cars

Position of the cars

In addition, the following data were developed for every locomotive in each division:

Number of miles run

Cost per mile for engineer and fireman

Gallons of oil used

Miles run to one pint (of oil)

Pounds of waste used

Pounds of tallow used

Cost for oil, waste, and tallow

Cost per mile for oil, waste, and tallow

Cost for repairs

Cost per mile run for repairs

Cords of fuel used

Cost per mile for fuel

Total cost for all the above items

Cost per ton per mile for the same

These data were then compiled for individual divisions for the purpose of determining costs as a step in developing rates. But more importantly, to McCallum, he used these data to compare the performance of individual divisions with each other and other railroads of shorter length to point out "neglect and mismanagement which prevail, thus enabling us to remedy the defect." Clearly, this was to observe and measure decentralized operations rather than provide centralized, detailed control and coordination for system optimization.

The next step in the development of the McCallum management was the creation of a standard set of "budget" accounts for each division for comparison with actual performance. However, while McCallum and his central staff appeared to create a number of summaries, agglomerated on a divisional basis for all functions, it is not clear today that the system was used for more than individual accountability on a differentiated or functional basis. McCallum clearly made a major step forward in developing management information and using it to isolate operating variations and weaknesses. He also used it in discipline, but he personally was still the primary integrator of functions in the Erie organization, and as such, his system primarily provided a means for intense central control. While he intended for the individual field operating groups to exercise as much initiative in solving problems as possible, the system discouraged such initiative. In fact, the field units were to do no more than execute the directives of the headquarters in a highly disciplined way.

The innovations of the Erie were highly publicized, and by the latter half of the 1850s, McCallum's principles and procedures of management had had significant impact in all forms of business in the United States and several other countries, including the United Kingdom.[16]

Financial manipulations of a group of unscrupulous financiers on the Erie had brought innovation in management structure to a standstill in 1860 and McCallum soon retired. Thus, it was at this point that we have to turn to the Pennsylvania Railroad for further developments. In 1957 G.

Edgar Thomson adapted the McCallum-Erie structure for the Pennsylvania Railroad as its major phase of construction was drawing to a close. However, Thomson was soon to make a significant contribution: the introduction of the "line-staff" relationship.

The 1857 organization of the Pennsylvania Railroad is reconstructed in figure 4-6. It can be seen that the financial and control functions were recognized as separate areas under the treasurer and controller. The Pennsylvania organization, like the Erie organization was divided into geographical divisions. However, the division superintendent directed the daily activities of essentially all of the maintenance of way, maintenance of equipment, and transportation employees in his division on the Pennsylvania. The master of machinery, master of transportation, and chief engineer had only indirect control of these functions by setting rules and standards for the "discipline and economy of conducting the business." This represented a major shift from the Erie, where there were three monolithic functional groups, with only the transportation group subdivided geographically as divisions. In the Pennsylvania, the chief officer of the function no longer had direct line responsibility, but had become a staff officer setting standards and procedures and providing consulting to the other officers and division employees as called on by the division superintendents.

Obviously, this was not a pattern of management relationship that was easily accepted. For brief periods (for example in 1866) there were signs of shifting of the balance between line and staff powers of the functional officers. However, by the 1880s this question had been resolved in favor of maintaining the integrity of the line of authority of the division superintendent and the functional officers acknowledged their role as staff.[17] This became the prototype of the Type II organization described in chapter 1.

To complete the examination of experiments in organization in the larger American railroads at mid-nineteenth century, it is necessary to turn to the New York Central Railroad.

The New York Central, unlike the B&O, Erie, and Pennsylvania, was not constructed as a single business enterprise. It was an assembly of ten short lines that were merged by financiers and politicians who had little experience (or perhaps interest) in the problems of integrating and coordinating the activities of the individual units. Primary attention was devoted to the legal and financial aspects of the consolidation. As a result, an organization developed as an evolutionary process rather than the self-conscious design of highly skilled and concerned engineers such as occurred on the other trunk railroads. This led to what might be called an organization of least resistance or convenience. Although the railroad was divided into five regional divisions, the "deputy" superintendent in each region had little or no power. The control of all activities rested in the hands of

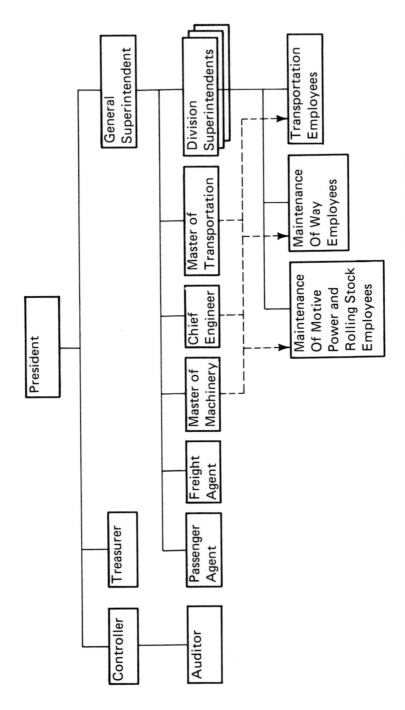

Figure 4-6. Organization of the Pennsylvania Railroad, 1857

Chauncy Vibbard, the general superintendent. Vibbard was heavily involved in activities outside the railroad, including the operation of a large liquor business in New York City and his duties as a congressman. As a result of these distractions, and his inability to exercise control of the activities of the railroad, strong autonomous functional departments developed at the headquarters. These functional groups appear to have jealously guarded their own empires. The divisional deputies barely had authority to operate the trains in their own divisions. The resulting structure closely resembled the "departmental" type of organization of the British railways that had evolved under Huish and his desire for centralization. When the Vanderbilts took control of the New York Central, they began to sharpen definitions of authority and delegation of authority to prevent collapse of the company.[18]

Solidification of the Railroad Management Style

The period of the mid-1860s through 1900 saw a rationalization and consolidation of the railroads. But, this occurred only after a period of very intense competition and economic struggle. This competitive period was to add two features to the structures of railroad organizations that had not been clearly defined previously: the financial and legal function and the traffic function.

As competition among the eastern railroads developed to a high pitch, two solutions were attempted to maintain relative competitive balance. The first was a series of interrailroad agreements and alliances. The second was rate cutting.

The development of interrailroad alliances led to a highly structured, centralized financial-legal department to coordinate the complex interrelationships between companies. As might be expected, given the highly independent personalities of the early chief executives of the railroads, agreements to limit competition or divide freight revenues were very unstable. Some interlocking ownership was practical to accomplish a measure of stability. The divergent personalities of Harriman, Gould, the Vanderbilts, Morgan, the Astors, the Belmonts, and others simply did not lend themselves to cooperation. However, the highly centralized financial organizations were developed for the purpose of providing rapid access to information and highly confidential transactions. Tight control of liquid assets and investment has continued as a feature of the modern railroad.

Centralized traffic functions developed to provide rapid system response to rate cutting and interline agreements among the competitors. Since the competition (on rare cases of agreement) tended to be on a systemic basis, it was natural that a centralized function be developed. The traffic function at this stage was apparently little more than rate setting. Personal selling, development of new services, and other promotion were considered to be strictly secondary in affecting consumer (shipper) behavior, and were essentially omitted from the competitive strategy. This led to a minimization of the field selling function, with local agents becoming little more than messengers for the traffic or rate managers.

In the years after the creation of the Interstate Commerce Commission (ICC) in 1887, the centralized traffic function became heavily involved in establishing rates and maintaining relationships with the commission. Because of this relationship and requirements for highly specialized quasi-legal training in conducting this function, it became increasingly less practical for a lay person to handle the traffic function. This further reinforced the high degree of centralization of traffic. As a corollary, the separation and differentiation of the traffic and operating functions developed further.

By the turn of the century, the conventional wisdom of railroad organizations was well established, as evidenced by the railroad observers of the period. We are fortunate to have the state of American railroads carefully documented in 1904 by Neville Priestly, under secretary to the Government of India, Railway Department. This manager observer, trained in the British railroad tradition, was sent to America to observe the railroads "with the view of studying the methods of working." He elected to interpret his assignment in the broadest sense and studied the United States industry in several dimensions, which he reported in great detail in his report *Organisation and Working of Railways in America.*[19]

Figure 4-7 reconstructs Priestly's verbal description of standards (or prototypical) organization of a railroad operating in excess of 1,000 miles. This organization, which closely resembles the Pennsylvania Railroad structure in figure 4-6, reflects an additional geographic subdivision, the district that was not present in the earlier Erie organization shown in figure 4-5.[20]

These districts were generally defined on the basis of several factors, including the nature of the country traversed, the density of the traffic, and the number of stations of importance.[21] Districts of as much as 500 miles were observed, but only in cases where there was only one station or terminal of importance. Although not mentioned explicitly by Priestly, districts were also defined by the type of steam locomotive required in a terrain. Steam locomotives, unlike the modern diesel locomotives that deliver full horsepower over a wide range of different speeds, were designed capable of delivering maximum power only at full design speed. Thus, different locomotive types were required for most efficient operation in mountain areas as compared with flat lands. Districts were established to

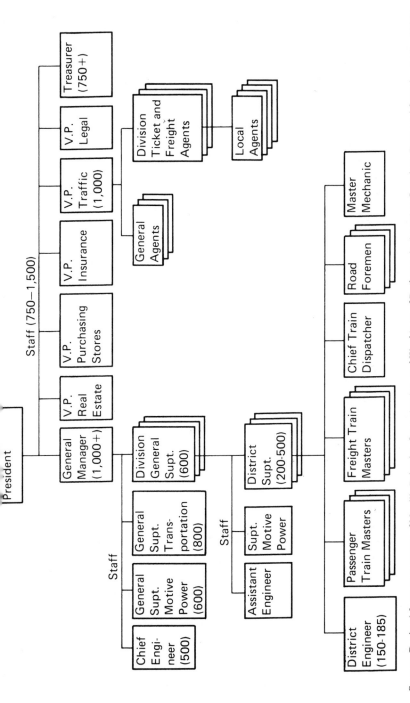

Figure 4-7. Conventional Railroad Organization Structure, Reconstructed From Priestly, 1904

Source: Derived from statements of Neville Priestly, *Organisation and Workings of Railways in America* (London: Eyre and Spottiswoode, 1904).

Note: Figures in parenthesis indicate approximate level of monthly compensation.

concentrate these engines in certain districts' roundhouses, notwithstanding other factors.

Staff officers in Priestly description, were seen to support the activities of the line officers (general manager, division general superintendents, and district superintendents) at each level. As a measure of the regard for ranks of individuals in the organization, the approximate monthly salary ranges for officers reported by Priestly are indicated in figure 4-7. In 1904 the average wages paid to railworkers was $600 per year, and $1,056 was the annual average salary paid to railroad and manufacturing clerical employees. It is fairly clear that the traffic manager was not slighted in the organization, but as Priestly commented, "the work [traffic] is never combined, as it is in India, with that of the transportation department, but is kept entirely separate, each department having its own organization all down the line."[22]

He does note some appreciation for operating problems by the traffic function in that: "The Traffic Officers are usually selected from members of the Operating Department and the station and goods staff who have shown a bias for this particular kind of work, as it is considered important that these officers should possess some knowledge of the incidence of the cost of transportation."[23] While this may have served as some basis for appreciating how costs are incurred in producing transportation, there is little evidence that there was any substantial integration of the operating and commercial functions.

Priestly observed that the apparent success of the American railroad management in the early twentieth century was the result of control through the organization, "statistics," inspection, training, and discipline. He found that great attention was devoted to the selection of officers. The criteria for selection appeard to be intelligence, good health, complete devotion to the company, sobriety, and high moral character.[24] Also, there appeared to be an implied requirement for self-control and personal discipline within a rigid system of company rules and directions (mostly originating from the staff officers). Tasks were broken into relatively small units that could be regularly measured and inspected. However, as Priestly described the situation:

. . . employees of every grade are allowed to conduct their business with as little interference as is possible. Everybody is believed to be honest until he has proved himself to be dishonest, and everyone is trusted until he has shown himself to be unworthy of confidence. All are judged by *results*. If these are not satisfactory, they are guided, and if there is still no improvement, they are changed.[25]

Priestly summarized the policy as: "Do what you please, but get the results and don't make too many mistakes. Hands-off everyone. Put the load on the man, and change him if he is unsuitable."[26]

There is evidence that this was indeed the practice. Measurement of performance was precise, expectations were high, and managers who failed were promptly removed from line positions. However, Priestly observed that if failure was due to causes that the manager could not reasonably be expected to control, another appointment was found or made for him, and a lateral transfer was made. So, while there was a hands-off policy, it was far from a relaxed or passive style of management. The operative parts of the policy were (1) frequent inspections of the operations and property, and (2) detailed management information reporting systems. Inspections were as infrequent as annually by the directors and general manager, and as frequent as monthly by district officers. These inspections were primarily oriented toward auditing the physical condition of the track, structures, and rolling stock. The management information systems (called statistics by Priestly) were the key to discipline. A brief consideration of what was measured (and rewarded) provides an insight into the behavior of the organization.

The primary report of the system was an abbreviated income statement. Such statements were constructed for the system, districts, and division levels. Joint costs and revenues were allocated between freight and passenger operations and between geographical subdivisions on a prorata basis by train miles. All expenses appear to have been calculated on a cash basis. There were no capital costs or depreciation expenses included in developing the "total expenses."[27] The division and district managers appear to have been measured on a practical cost center basis, assuming that labor and material expenditures were the accounts to be controlled.

Figures of average length of haul for freight and passengers were calculated, and revenue per ton mile of freight or passenger mile were developed, but there was no attempt to relate these to a profit center below the total system.

Other results were presented to provide a more complete understanding of the performance. These included:

Average mileage of road operated

Number of trains run. Passenger
Number of trains run. Freight

Train mileage. Passenger
Train mileage. Freight

Average potential load of a freight train

Average number of passengers per mile of road operated
Average number of tons of freight per mile of road operated
Average number of passengers per train per mile

Average number of tons of freight per train per mile

Vehicle mileage. Passenger

Vehicle mileage. Freight (loaded and empty separately)
> In the direction in which traffic preponderates.

Vehicle mileage. Freight (loaded and empty separately)''
> In reverse direction.

Vehicle mileage. Total of each

Average number of vehicles per train per mile—
  Passenger
  Freight, loaded
  Freight, empty
  Freight, total

Average number in each be vehicle per mile—
  Of passengers
  Of tons of freight per loaded vehicle
  Of tons of freight per vehicle, loaded and empty included

Average carrying capacity of a freight vehicle

Average cost of operation per passenger train

Average cost of operation freight train

Average cost of operation passenger vehicle

Average cost of operation freight vehicle

Average cost of operation passenger mile

Average cost of operation ton mile

Average number of engines in service

Number of trips run by all engines

Engine mileage

Engine service in hours. Potential

Engine service in hours. Actual

Engine service in hours. Miles per hour while in service.

Average cost of operation *per train per mile*, and average cost *per 100 tons one mile* of—
  Station service
  Train service
  Engine service

Contingencies

Maintenance of equipment

Maintenance of road and structures

General expenses

Total Operating Expenses[28]

There appeared to be only nominal attention devoted to the effective use of rolling stock. While there was some consideration of number of engines available for service and the number of trips performed, the report was silent on the issue of the level of miles per car month, revenue per car, or revenue per dollar of investment.

While the detailed and frequent report of the management information system was the heart of the discipline and control of the railroads, it stressed labor and material cost reduction as key management objectives; capital productivity was ignored; and profitability was assumed to derive automatically from economical practices regarding labor and material. This style of management was consistent with the belief that the manager had little control over prices. Part of this attitude certainly stemmed from the belief that division of revenue between passenger and freight operations and between individual geographic subdivisions was arbitrary and useless at best. Additionally, rates were established through the traffic department on the basis of monopoly or oligopoly pricing. As the pricing function passed under the regulation of the ICC nothing occurred to lead management to conclude that a division or district manager was any more capable of controlling the revenue portion of the profit calculation.

By the turn of the century the railroads in a period of approximately 50 years had undergone more experiences of dealing with radically different management problems than had been witnessed by any other business enterprises of the time. The initial steps were taken to establish some form of local management capable of directing and supervising a manageable piece of business activity. The natural evolution was to follow a pattern that permitted the maximum degree of central control of individual functions. However, given the limitation of the communications—telegraph and business car—it was necessary to subdivide operations into smaller operating units in which all functions reported to one manager. The staff function evolved to provide consistence of policy among the operations of geographical subdivisions. This style of organization became the standard railroad management structure and the basis of organization for many other businesses. But, in most respects, organizational innovation slowed greatly, and little was done to accommodate new competitive and technological environments after these creative beginnings.

Notes

1. T.R. Gourvish, *Mark Huish and the London and North Western Railway* (Leicester: Leicester University Press, 1972), p. 31.

2. Ibid., pp. 32-33.

3. Ibid., p. 30.

4. Ibid., p. 27.

5. Ibid., p. 22.

6. Ibid., p. 22.

7. Ibid., p. 22.

8. Ibid., p. 27.

9. Ibid., p. 106.

10. Ibid., p. 112.

11. Ibid., p. 172.

12. D. Daryl Wyckoff, *Organizational Formality and Performance in the Motor-Carrier Industry* (Lexington, Mass.: Lexington Books, D.C. Heath and Company, 1974), pp. 59-63.

13. Alfred D. Chandler, Jr. and Stephen Salsbury, "The Railroads: Innvators in Modern Business Administration," in *The Railroad and the Space Program: An Exploration in Historical Analogy*, ed. Bruce Mazlish (Cambridge, Mass.: M.I.T. Press, 1965), pp. 127-30. Alfred D. Chandler, "The Railroads: Pioneers in Modern Corporate Management, *Business History Review*, Spring 1965, pp. 16-19.

14. Chandler and Salsbury, "Innovators," pp. 131-34.

15. Ibid., pp. 135-37; Chandler, "Pioneers," pp. 22-27.

16. Chandler and Salsbury, "Innovators," pp. 138-40; Chandler, "Pioneers," pp. 27-33; Daniel C. McCallum, "Superintendent's Report, March 25, 1856, *Annual Report of the New York and Erie Railroad Company for 1855* in *The Railroads: The Nation's First Big Business*, ed. Alfred D. Chandler, Jr. (New York: Harcourt Brace and World, Inc., 1965), pp. 101-8. Alfred D. Chandler, Jr. *Henry Varnum Poor: Business Editor, Analysts, and Reformer* (Cambridge, Mass.: Harvard University Press, 1956), pp. 144-53.

17. Chandler and Salsbury, "Innovators," pp. 140-41; Chandler, "Pioneers," pp. 33-36.

18. Chandler and Salsbury, "Innovators," pp. 141- 43.

19. Neville Priestley, *Organisation and Working of Railways in America* (London: Eyre and Spottiswoode, 1904).

20. Ibid., p. 4.

21. Ibid., p. 13.
22. Ibid., p. 6.
23. Ibid., p. 6.
24. Ibid., pp. 15-16.
25. Ibid., p. 10.
26. Ibid., p. 11.
27. Ibid., pp. 26-29.
28. Ibid., p. 29-30.

5 Loss of Adaptiveness

Since the turn of the century railroads have demonstrated a general pattern of low adaptiveness in behavior and a limited variety of responses to their environment. It is a gross overgeneralization and too simplistic to state flatly that a substantial portion of present railroad behavior and attitudes have their origins in actions taken several decades ago. But, there is substantial truth in this statement, as seen in the present railroad organizations and attitudes towards competitors, customers, and regulators. Without attempting to evaluate further the performance of railroad organizations, which is discussed at length in chapter 6, I want to focus here one possible response these firms might have made to changes in their environment: adjustment in organizational structures.

In my research I found it difficult to determine whether: (1) the stability (or stagnation) of the organizations was a major contributor to the lack of the railroads' responsiveness to environmental changes, or (2) the stability of the organizations was simply an indication of this behavior. In other words, was there a cause and effect relationship? I am not sure that I have an answer to this question, but the evidence clearly indicates a strong association between these two observations. In fact, as a result of this research, I am prepared to state that the stability of railroad organizations and loss of adaptiveness were interrelated and reinforced each other.

For the past seven decades, there have been few changes in railroad management organizations. This would seem improbable under the contingency organization theory, given the considerable changes that have occurred during that period in the market, and the competitive, regulatory, labor, and technological environments. While the railroad organizations appeared to be particularly appropriate at the beginning of the twentieth century, it is difficult to believe that this is still true. In fact, a process occurred that essentially reinforced the existence of the organization by those in it. Outside inputs were often ignored or suppressed. Rather than being change seekers, the railroads attempted to accommodate the changing environment by retarding the change or accommodating the new situation with minimum change to the way business was conducted. This is not an unusual action. Most organisms, whether they be biological or business firms, attempt to make minor modifications to adjust to such changes in their environment. But in the case of the railroads, perhaps because of their great power, arrogance, or monopolistic history, they seemed to demonstrate a belief that they could change the environment.

Of course, if this is the belief, there is little justification to change the organization. The failure to change the organization appeared to reinforce the attitude that the environment could be made to conform to the railroads. This led to a vicious circle, which has made change increasingly more difficult with each passing year.

My observations indicate that this loss of adaptiveness stems from an attitude that has been building in the railroad industry. However, several railroad managers I interviewed made strong arguments that it is simply a product of the type of organization that has been so broadly preserved in the industry. The preservation of this organizational form (Types I and II, described in chapter 1) stems from several features of the industry.

Arguments Supporting the Universality of the Present Railroad Organization

The railroad managers I interviewed put forth the following arguments in support of the universality and stability of railroad organizations since the turn of the century: First, the technology of railroading is so overwhelmingly a significant factor and has changed so little that it has dictated the organization. This is reinforced by geographic and joint-cost/joint-product natures of the process that have not provided easy opportunities to decentralize profit responsibility. Second, the solidarity of the labor organizations serving nearly all of the companies in the industry has tended to induce unified behavior and similar operating rules among the companies. Third, members of the industry have found that unified reaction or interaction with the ICC as the industry regulator has tended to lead to a single approach to problem solving. Fourth, the heavy interdependence and high volume of connecting operations between railroads has led to a high degree of standardization.

Certainly, all of these factors have contributed to maintaining the same railroad organizations with little change over several decades. But, even more important, the managers themselves felt these were vital reasons that justified this, and here is the beginning of an attitude that accepted organization and management behavior as essentially invariable. Today, after several decades of this behavior by managers, and reinforcement of this attitude, there is a large population of railroad employees who were selected, trained, promoted, and rewarded on the basis of these beliefs. I believe these factors are true, but seriously question whether they are the overwhelming barriers to change that they might appear to be to the railroaders. But, I do not doubt the magnitude of the barrier presented by the attitudes and training of thousands of railroaders who accept them as truths.

To determine the probability of individual companies and managers transcending this attitude and situation, it is necessary to examine their sources and causes. The question that concerns me is, has the "railroad socialization" process become so effective and ingrained in the industry as to make it impractical to adjust the management styles and organizations to fit the changes in the railroads' tasks. I refer to this condition of attitude as *organizational stagnation*.

Causes of Stagnation

A well-worn path of watchful waiting has often characterized the career path to the top of railroad management. Railroads are accused of placing greater premiums on the junior manager who patiently waits out the complex and inflexible seniority system than on one who demonstrates impatient and aggressive talent and energy for solving problems. The railroads, the first businesses to cope with the management of large enterprises, were also the first businesses to face the problems of dealing with the creeping atrophy and ossification of a maturing industry of large scale. A systemic and technologically complex process, railroad operations easily lend themselves to an apprentice (craft) training system. A maturing industry, such as the railroads have been for several decades, in which the need for higher ranking managers was leveling off or falling, combined with promotion from within generated by the apprentice training system, was ripe for the development of a "safe" (informal, but well-understood) seniority system to replace the merit system.[1]

It has been observed by some that railroad officers are older than those found in other industries, and these observers frequently state that this has contributed significantly to stagnation. Examining tables 5-1 and 5-2, there is some evidence to suggest that railroad officers are older than the officers of transportation companies in general and all other companies. However, when companies of size comparable with railroads are considered, there is no consistent evidence of a striking difference. So, it is not clear that the age of the officers is a major factor.

Table 5-3 compares the ages of the managers in various departments with the ages of the top officers. Since I have not found such data for other industries, it is difficult to comment whether railroads are different on this point. There does not seem to be an unreasonable separation or generation gap between middle and top managers. But, there is a possible

Table 5-1
Comparison of Age of Chief Officers in Various Industries (Percent)

Presidents (1972)

Age	Railroads[a]	Transportation	Insurance	Banking	Utilities	Merchandise	Financial	Other	All Companies	Industrial Companies
20-29	—	—	—	—	—	—	—	b	—	—
30-39	—	3.6	—	2.9	—	3.6	2.9	b	1.9	2.0
40-49	10.0	17.9	23.5	22.9	28.9	14.3	22.9	b	24.8	26.1
50-59	65.0	57.1	55.9	45.7	50.0	78.5	45.7	b	56.9	57.2
60+	25.0	24.1	20.6	28.5	21.2	3.6	28.5	b	16.4	14.7

Chief Marketing Executive (1971)

Age	Railroads[a]	Transportation	Insurance	Banking	Utilities	Merchandise	Financial	Other	All Companies	Industrial Companies
20-29	—	—	—	4.2	—	b	b	b	—	1.0
30-39	5.0	—	5.3	25.0	—	b	b	b	4.9	9.0
40-49	30.0	45.0	26.3	37.5	34.6	b	b	b	42.7	39.3
50-59	55.0	45.0	47.4	29.1	42.3	b	b	b	42.7	39.8
60+	10.0	10.0	21.0	4.2	23.1	b	b	b	9.7	10.9

Chief Financial Executive (1970)

Age	Railroads[a]	Transportation	Insurance	Banking	Utilities	Merchandise	Financial	Other	All Companies	Industrial Companies
20-29	—	—	—	b	—	—	b	b	—	—
30-39	—	19.0	4.0	b	3.0	4.0	b	4.0	8.0	11.0
40-49	33.3	24.0	7.0	b	27.0	41.0	b	36.0	28.0	35.0
50-59	40.0	43.0	56.0	b	46.0	51.0	b	46.0	53.0	45.0
60+	26.9	14.0	33.0	b	34.0	4.0	b	14.0	11.0	9.0

Note: Columns may not add to 100 percent due to rounding.

[a]From a study of 20 major railroads in 1971. All other data from studies by Heidrick and Struggles, Inc.

[b]Not available.

Table 5-2
Comparison of Ages of Chief Officers by Company Revenues (Percent)

Presidents (1972)

Age	Railroads[a]	Transportation	All Companies	0.165-0.269	0.270-0.449	0.500-1.00	>1.00
					Annual Revenues, $ Billions		
20-29	—	—	—	—	—	—	—
30-39	—	3.6	1.9	4.0	1.2	2.5	—
40-49	10.0	17.9	24.8	27.6	24.4	30.0	22.1
50-59	65.0	57.1	56.0	56.6	65.9	55.0	50.0
60+	25.0	24.1	16.4	11.8	8.5	12.5	27.9

Chief Marketing Executives (1971)

Age	Railroads[a]	Transportation	All Companies	<0.300	0.300-0.700	>0.700
					Annual Revenues, $ Billions	
20-29	—	—	—	—	—	—
30-39	5.0	—	4.9	14.0	12.0	7.0
40-49	30.0	45.0	42.7	46.0	31.0	38.0
50-59	55.0	45.0	42.7	43.0	48.0	45.0
60+	10.0	10.0	9.7	7.0	9.0	10.0

Chief Financial Executives (1970)

Age	Railroads[a]	Transportation	All Companies	<0.250	0.250-0.500	>0.500
					Annual Revenues, $ Billions	
20-29	—	—	—	—	—	—
30-39	—	19.0	8.0	14.0	12.0	7.0
40-49	33.3	24.0	28.0	46.0	31.0	38.0
50-59	40.0	43.0	53.0	43.0	48.0	45.0
60+	26.7	14.0	11.0	7.0	9.0	10.0

Note: Columns may not add to 100 percent due to rounding.

[a]From a study of the officers of 20 major railroads in 1971. All other data from studies by Heidrick and Struggles, Inc.
[b]Columns may not add to 100 percent due to rounding.

Table 5-3
Comparison of Ages of Railroad Managers and Chief Officers by Department

Age	Railroad Managers[a]	Presidents[b]
	Executive Departments	
20-29	4.0	—
30-39	13.0	—
40-49	34.0	10.0
50-59	44.0	65.0
60 +	5.0	25.0

Age	Railroad Managers[a]	Chief Operating Officers[b]
	Operating Departments	
20-29	6.0	—
30-39	18.0	—
40-49	38.0	33.3
50-59	30.0	50.0
60 +	8.0	16.7

Age	Railroad Managers[a]	Chief Marketing Officers[b]
	Marketing Departments	
20-29	8.0	—
30-39	18.0	5.0
40-49	36.0	30.0
50-59	33.0	55.0
60 +	5.0	10.0

Age	Railroad Managers[a]	Chief Marketing Officers[b]
	Finance Departments	
20-29	c	—
30-39	c	—
40-49	c	33.3
50-59	c	40.0
60 +	c	26.7

Note: Columns may not add to 100 percent due to rounding.

[a]Derived from "Decision Makers 1974," *Modern Railroads*, October, 1974.
[b]From a study of the officers of 20 major railroads in 1971.
[c]Not available.

lack of individuals in middle management in the categories under age 40. This certainly may contribute to the impression that railroad management is "old" in the eyes of the young management candidate.

While it may not be entirely justified, I have observed a perception among young railroaders that top management is a "closed shop." This perception is much stronger than I have observed in most other industries, but most closely resembles attitudes I have observed in some utilities companies and government agencies. This attitude has led to behavior that holds tradition in high esteem and acceptance of conventional wisdom well past its usefulness. Herein lies one of the primary causes of the stagnation of the railroad management, the inflexibility of thinking and rationalization of failure in a fatalistic acceptance of the situation. How did this develop?

The railroad industry, even in the 1970s, is a large employer of people. But, the number of employees in the American Class I railroads was only 520,000 in 1973, down from a high of 2 million in 1920.[2] During the earliest days of the industry in the late nineteenth century, the railroads were faced with the difficult problems of recruiting, training, and retaining a large number of middle managers to direct the army of people who operated their geographically widespread facilities. By 1885 the *Biographical Director of Railroad Officials of America* reported that there were about 600,000 men employed by the railroads under the direction of approximately 5,000 general and division officers.[3]

By the end of the nineteenth century, railroad officers often had status that was similar to that of doctors, lawyers, bankers, and successful merchants. They were considered to be financially well rewarded, and were observed to have a mark of dignity. By 1910 the list of "officials and superintendents," which roughly corresponded to the earlier 1885 category mentioned above, had increased from 5,000 to 20,000. The rate of growth in this group had peaked at 32,426 in 1920.[4] While the second category was more broadly defined than the 1885 list, the important point to note is the leveling-off process.

The structure of the general classes of railroad employees is shown in table 5-4. As can be seen, enginemen and conductors were paid relatively well. But, as one observer commented in 1906, "The railway industry has not produced many millionaires, but it offers steady employment at reasonable rates of remuneration."

The earliest managers of the railroads, as can be seen from chapter 4, were innovative general entrepreneurs with many business interests. Many of the top managers entered railroading from other occupations, including general business, military, and construction. However, most of the superintendents described in chapter 4 in the developing organizations

Table 5-4
General Classes of Railroad Employees, 1900 and 1910

		1900			1910	
Employees	Number	Per 100 Miles of Line	Average Daily Compensation	Number	Per 100 Miles of Line[a]	Average Daily Compensation
General officers	4,916	3	$10.45	5,476	2	$13.27
Other officers	4,669	2	5.22	9,392	4	6.22
General office clerks	32,265	17	2.19	76,329	32	2.40
Station agents	31,610	16	1.75	37,379	16	2.12
Other station men	89,831	47	1.60	153,104	64	1.84
Enginemen	42,837	22	3.75	64,691	27	4.55
Firemen	44,130	23	2.14	68,321	28	2.74
Conductors	29,957	16	3.17	48,682	20	3.91
Other trainmen	74,274	39	1.96	136,938	57	2.69
Machinists	32,831	17	2.30	55,193	23	3.08
Carpenters	46,666	24	2.04	68,085	28	2.51
Other shopmen	114,773	60	1.73	225,196	94	2.18
Section foremen	33,085	17	1.68	44,207	18	1.99
Other trackmen	226,799	118	1.22	378,955	157	1.47
Switch tenders, crossing tenders, and watchmen	50,789	26	1.80	44,682	19	1.69
Telegraph operators and dispatchers	25,218	13	1.96	42,435	18	2.33
Employees—account floating equipment	7,597	4	1.92	10,549	4	2.22
All other employees and laborers	125,386	65	1.71	229,806	95	2.01
Total	1,017,633	529		1,699,420	706	

Source: Adapted from Interstate Commerce Commission. *Twenty-third Annual Report on the Statistics of Railways, June 3, 1910* (Washington, D.C.: 1912), pp. 33, 34, 38; Reprinted in Stuart Morris, "Stalled Professionalism: The Recruitment of Railway Officials in the United States, 1885-1940," *Business History Review*, Autumn 1973.

[a]Does not cover switching and terminal companies.

were "home-grown" managers from the ranks of operating personnel of the railroads themselves.

As can be noted in table 5-5, the beginning railroad occupations of individuals who had achieved senior positions in management changed considerably from 1885 to 1913. For example, 18.4 percent began in senior positions (presumably having entered railroading by some lateral move from outside the industry) in 1885. However, by 1913 and as late as 1940, these figures had dropped to 4.8 and 5.2 percent respectively. This hints at the process of closing off the opportunities to those outside the railroad system. The one category that moved against this trend is that of "attorneys and assistant counsels." In 1885 this was the entry point for only 0.2

Table 5-5
Beginning Occupations of Railroad Officials, 1885 through 1940

Beginning Occupation	1885		1913		1940	
	Number out of 500	Percent	Number out of 500	Percent	Number out of 500	Percent
Senior positions (excluding trustees and directors except chairmen of the board)	92	18.4	24	4.8	26	5.2
Clerks (including book-keepers, stenographers, and ticket clerks)	148	29.6	182	36.4	201	40.2
Messengers and office boys (including station helpers)	31	6.2	50	10.0	48	9.6
Telegraph operators	40	8.0	55	11.0	39	7.8
Agents (station, local general, freight, passenger, and travelling)	29	5.8	15	3.0	16	3.2
Combined clerical and commercial first employment	248	49.6	302	60.4	304	60.8
"Assistant engineers" (mainly rodmen and chainmen) and draftsmen (civil)	58	11.6	62	12.4	68	13.6
Machinist apprentices (including "special apprentices")	31	6.2	40	8.0	31	6.2
Brakemen (and firemen)	21	4.2	14	2.8	4	0.8
Laborers, sectionmen	14	2.8	4	0.8	7	1.4
Attorneys assistant counsels	1	0.2	11	2.2	16	3.2
Miscellaneous	35	7.0	43	8.6	44	8.8
Total	500	100.0	500	100.0	500	100.0

Source: Stuart Morris, "Stalled Professionalism: The Recruitment of Railway Officials in the United States, 1885-1940," *Business History Review*, Autumn 1973.

percent of senior officials, but this grew to 2.2 and 3.2 percent in 1913 and 1940. This partially reflects the increasing demands placed on the railroads to cope with the complexities of the quasi-legal system of ICC regulation and other government entanglements that many railroads have found themselves in as a result of their financial difficulties and frequent bankruptcies.

The general category of "combined clerical and commercial" shifted from 49.6 to 60.8 percent in the period of 1885 to 1940. However, this categorization may be slightly deceptive. There is little evidence that there were many people in commercial (marketing) positions that achieved senior positions. The most significant changes occurred in the subgroup "clerks." This group was the entry point for as few as 29.4 percent of the senior officials in 1885, but steadily increased to 40.2 percent in 1940.

Simply looking at the entry point of the career path of senior officials may not be the most satisfactory means of describing the entire trajectory; however, it provides important clues to how the process of management development has operated in the railroad industry. Table 5-5 cannot stand alone; it is necessary to look behind these figures to understand better the impact of a system that has drawn so heavily on its pool of "clerks" and "assistant engineers" for senior officials. As one observer noted, "There was generally only one generation of managing engineers (formally educated in civil engineering) on a railroad; with their passing the young men who had grown up in the service and were without any special education took their places. . . . The effect of this was to produce the 'practical man' who had little use for anything to be learned in a school."[5]

Attitudes Toward Formal Education

The middle managers of the railroads had to be hardy and prepared to deal with dangerous and physically demanding operating conditions. They were expected to manage a work force that was often a "rough and tumble" group of men.[6]

While individuals with advanced education might not have been systematically excluded from railroad management, they found little to encourage them. Advanced education, in the classical sense, provided little or no comparative advantage to the individual in front line or middle management positions on most railroads, compared to what such an asset might yield in other situations.[7] There was even evidence that the educated man was put upon and ridiculed by other middle managers and the workers.[8] The primary example of the exception to this appeared in the hiring of formally educated civil engineers into positions of responsibility in the maintenance of way and structure deparments. However, while such positions seemed to have satisfied some desire for achieving professional predominance, for many years they also tended to be dead-end situations in terms of a career path to top positions for most engineers, according to some observers.[9]

The education that was most valuable to the ambitious, potential railroad manager in the United States was that derived from on-the-job operating experience. The question is whether this is the most effective way for the young manager to gain this experience today, and whether the time consumed in the on-the-job training process discourages graduates from formal education programs from entering the process or preempts those who are in the process from broadening their knowledge and base of experience.

In the 1920s it was proposed that an educational program that combined the features of a cadet system with a technical and trade school education be developed to short-cut the less efficient, on-the-job training process. Professor W.J. Cunningham, then the James J. Hill Professor of Transportation at the Harvard Business School, had hoped to develop a cadet program, together with practical general management and business administration training. While there were great expectations for such a program, they were never realized. The railroads themselves failed to support the program, and the schools found that there was a greater demand for their graduates in more receptive markets in other industries. Few individuals that graduated from Cunningham's programs or other university programs ever went on to become railroad officers.[10] This may be because such programs never fully developed in the directions that were originally envisioned. While they might have been counted as not being highly successful in swelling the ranks of railroad management, they have populated the organizations of some of the most successful and creative business enterprises in the world. Railroad management was simply not prepared to accept this substitution of formal training for "experiential" training.

It would seem likely that it would have been possible to design an educational program that would have provided the necessary technical and craft training without retaining the heavy dependence on the more traditional apprentice system. The failure appears to stem from three sources: First, the educators had one idea of what education was necessary or desirable that clearly was not consistent with what railroad managers felt was of value. The educators failed to provide what the practitioners required and failed to sell the value of what they were providing. Specifically, the educators wanted to teach conceptual material, such as economics, which might prepare the students for broader horizons to the almost total exclusion of teaching the trade. While the broadening might have produced several generations of more flexible and adaptive managers, they were almost certain to have been doomed to failure for a lack of the basic technical knowledge of the craft. Second, the men in the industry who had already "made the grade" seemed to view formal education as a sly attempt to avoid passing through the initiation rites of being an assistant train master and other first-line experiences that many of them had endured. Third, because many managers who had made the grade had little formal education, they believed that it was not necessary for success, and discounted its potential value because they never understood what it might add. However, even more distressing is the fact that some officers who lacked formal education felt threatened by candidates with such training.

Of course, it would be absurd to suggest that there are no railroad officers with advanced, formal, professional, business training or that all railroads have failed to provide such education for promising candidates within their own companies. This is not the case. There are numerous examples of highly educated and formally trained railroad officers. I am familiar with several railroads who regularly support the training of their employees at university programs, such as the intensive three-month, middle and advanced management programs at the Harvard Business School. But, these efforts and individuals often fail to make as much impact as might be hoped for. Quite often, such education is for individuals who are already set in their ways. In some companies, attendance at such executive training is considered as a reward for previous adherence to company values and conventional wisdom rather than an opportunity for a learning experience. But, perhaps the most distressing observation that I made during my research was an outright appearance of anti-intellectualism and a sense of embarrassment at times about having formal education among some middle managers. One was more free to talk about operating "war stories" than intellectual pursuits or attainments.

There appears to be a need to play the role of the hard-working young man "climbing the ladder" in the great railroad tradition of the journalistic accounts of "rising from the ranks, romantic life stories of fine great railroaders who began at the bottom—track laborers, wood choppers, surveyors, and car builders who have climbed to the top of great systems."[11] The pretense of the maintenance of such a system might not do any harm. The problem is, the tradition is perceived by railroad managers and potential candidates as having a reality. This in itself tends to make it real, and herein is the danger.

Besides possibly limiting the horizons and flexibility of railroad managers, which is a serious defect, this attitude tends to reinforce the apprentice and seniority system and closes the door to opportunities to challenge the conventional wisdom of earlier generations.

Other Factors Contributing to Stagnation

Railroaders tend to be clannish. They appear to feel more secure with other railroaders. The source of this attitude may have been the transitory relationship of many railroaders to communities in which they lived. Because railroaders, particularly operating personnel and managers, were transferred to new locations frequently, a social system and a behavior centered around the railroad and other employees of the railroad developed. This was not only true among the employees, but it also extended to their families. This is not a situation that is unique to railroads. I have observed the same transitory and group identification behavior among families in the armed forces and American employees and their families stationed in the Middle Eastern oil production areas. Certainly the forces leading to clannishness are clear in both of these cases, but behavior similar to this was observed among the employees and families of larger firms that frequently transfer managers such as IBM Corporation and General Electric Corporation.[12] While this is not a unique feature of railroads, it cannot be ignored. This strong identification between railroaders and their companies and fellow employees, which was described so vividly by William Frederick Cottrell in his book, *The Railroader*,[13] has developed to a new stage at present. Many of the railroaders I met demonstrated a defensive attitude about railroads and their behavior. This was particularly evident among individuals who had progressed through the ranks of middle management. This has led to an intensified reinforcement (or even rationalization) of the policy of promotion from within a railroad and other railroad actions and policies. This process has also contributed to an attitude of suspicion of any value or idea that is generated outside the system, and, as in many closed social systems, the belief that insiders are more worthy and trustworthy than outsiders and behavior that rejects anything "not invented here."

Watchful Waiting

"If a man has patience, what need has he for armor?" asked the philosopher Bhartrihari.[14] This might be good advice to the young candidate considering a career in railroad management. An informal version of the seniority system of the operating crafts in railroads was found to occur in the ranks of management as early as the first decade of the twentieth century. This policy has been articulated and defended in many ways, but one of the most direct statements of it that I found made clear the necessity of such a system to determine promotion in order to preserve "the morale of railway employees." This 1930 statement described this policy as "one of the most inspiring things in the industry."[15] When this statement was made, the average age of chief executives of traffic departments was 58, while the average age of *junior* traffic officers was 44, so there was already substantial evidence of the constriction of promotional opportunities as a result of the leveling off of the growth of the number of people in the industry and a diminishing need for administrative officers.

As pointed out by Stuart Morris, the situation could be relieved only by "recourse to seniority as the main arbitrator of advancement. The more remote the prospect of rapid promotion, the greater the demand for gradual promotion based on seniority."[16] As the seniority process became more functional, the hope for rapid promotion diminished. This, together with the evolution of departmentalism, described in chapter 4, tended to close down opportunities to a rigid process that was difficult to overcome and frequently brutal to the impatient candidate. For, while the movement upward was usually conditional on seniority, this was not sufficient. Upward mobility too often appeared to be based on the condition that the candidate continued to show that the socialization process of the organization had effectively occurred.

By 1942 Paul Dunn wrote, "The seniority principle also appears to have permeated into the official staff, as on many railroads little appreciable effort is made to overcome the tendency of seniority to obscure differences in individual [managers] capabilities."[17] He further observed, "the ingrowth of the seniority system" had developed "a rather fatalistic attitude on the part of railroad officers," since, being unable to promote men on ability during the early stages of their careers, they found it "difficult to groom promising prospects for the first step on the ladder of official promotion."

Or, as stated by the Temporary National Economic Committee in 1941 while investigating "Bureaucracy and Trusteeship in Large Corporations": "The idea of promotion by seniority permeated the railways all the way down the hierarchy, where men are apt to think more of the time in their records than on how effectively that time has been spent."[18]

This system self-selected men of patience, turning away or discouraging those whose impatient questioning and aggressiveness might have introduced a challenge to their seniors and conventional wisdom. The railroads might have profited more from men with more "armor" and willingness to be aggressive and less patient.

A More Optimistic Note

This chapter has offered an explanation why railroad management organizations have tended to stagnate and management behavior has become less adaptive and vigorous over the past several decades. It has also set a very discouraging tone for the hopes of change because of the massive size of the organizations and the deep-seated internalization of the attitudes described.

However, there appears to be some indication that some changes are in the wind. First, while it is difficult to measure, there are some data to suggest that the average ages of executives in the transportation industries, including railroads, are coming down. Second, I have observed several railroads that have broken with tradition and appointed officers from outside the railroad industry to top management positions within the past three years. These appointments were specifically made to stimulate new approaches and thinking. Third, railroads appear to be taking a more aggressive position on training middle managers in general management outside the more conventional in-house and on-the-job trainig programs that tend to reinforce intracompany and industry viewpoints, values, and approaches. The question is, are these steps too small and too late?

Notes

1. Stuart Morris "Stalled Professionalism: The Recruitment of Railway Officials in the United States, 1885-1940." *Business History Review*, Autumn 1973, p. 322.

2. *Moody's Transportation Manual* (New York: Moody's Investors Service, 1967), p. 39. Also see, *Railroad Facts* (Washington D.C.: Association of American Railroads, 1974), p. 58.

3. *Biographical Directory of the Railway Officials of America* (Chicago and New York, 1885).

4. Morris, "Stalled Professionalism," p. 320.

5. J. Shirley Easton, "Educational Training for Railway Service," *Report of The Commissioner of Education* (Washington, D.C.: U.S. Government, 1900), p. 875. Also see W. Frederick Cottrell, *The Railroader* (Stanford, Calif.: Stanford University Press, 1940). pp. 7 and 16.

6. Cottrell, *The Railroader*, p. 11.

7. M.J. Gormley, "Railroading as a Career for College Men," *Railway Age*, June 21, 1930, p. 16.

8. Morris, "Stalled Professionalism," p. 327.

9. Ibid., pp. 326-28.

10. Ibid., pp. 329-30. Also see "Training Understudies for Official Positions," *Railway Age*, February 26, 1927, pp. 574-76; also see John Hays Gardiner, *Harvard* (New York: Oxford University Press, 1914), p. 221.

11. "Rising From the Ranks," *The Railroad Man's Magazine*, November 1906, p. 481.

12. William H. White, Jr. *The Organization Man* (Garden City, New York: Doubleday and Co., Inc., 1956), pp. 162 and 304-5.

13. Cottrell, *The Railroader*, pp. 42-59.

14. Bhartrihari, *Nite Sataka No. 21*.

15. Gormley "Railroading as a Career," p. 16.

16. Morris, "Stalled Professionalism," p. 330.

17. Paul C. Dunn, *Selection and Training of Railroad Supervisors* (Cambridge, Mass.: Harvard University Press, 1942), p. 37.

18. Temporary National Economic Committee, *Monograph II, Bureaucracy and Trusteeship in Large Corporations* (Washington, D.C., U.S. Government, 1941), p. 50.

6 Performance of Present Railroad Organizations

It is not my purpose to dwell on the state of the United States railroad industry. There is little argument with the observation that, "Railroading has been a troubled industry for half a century. The troubles have approached the crisis stage once again during the past few years. . . ."[1] Bankruptcies abound and the railroads appear to be incapable of handling the surges of traffic that have led analysts to speak of the "profitless booms" that have brought more grief than relief to the industry. On one side, shippers are speaking out in fear of the prospect of loss of railroad service; yet shippers' decisions based on railroad performance contribute to the general erosion of the industry's market share of the most attractive freight.[2]

The so-called railroad problem is complex and multifaceted. The purpose of this analysis is to concentrate on the features of the performance of railroads': (1) ability to transact operations in a cost effective manner, and (2) ability to respond to the environment (primarily market and competitive) in a flexible and responsive fashion.

Ability to Transact

Railroads are highly systemic operations. An imbalance of traffic in one portion of a company may completely disrupt the entire operation. Unlike some manufacturers whose individual operations are not dependent on each other, the railroad system may fail as the result of the failure of any part. Like any process that is highly dependent on balance, the railroad is relatively inflexible, and changes are highly disruptive, thus discouraging changes and innovations. This systemic feature also results in the need for a high degree of coordination between the individual elements. Also, the systemic character of railroads have made them logical targets for systems analysts who delight in "optimal" engineering solutions to systems balancing. Unfortunately such solutions tend to be difficult for static situations because of their scale and overwhelming problems for dynamic solutions.

The intercity portion of railroad activity is fraught with joint costs that arise from this systemic situation. It is extremely difficult to assign costs to individual movements without a high degree of arbitrary allocation.

Table 6-1

Comparison of Ratios of Selected Expenditures to Revenue of Railroads with Other Industries, 1971

Industry Group	SIC	Cost of Materials	Payroll All Employees	Annual Capital Expenditures
Food and kindred products	20	0.6733	0.1115	0.0216
Chemicals and allied products	28	0.4335	0.1592	0.0566
Petroleum and coal products	29	0.7967	0.0580	0.0648
Rubber and plastic products	30	0.4425	0.2514	0.0424
Fabricated metal products	34	0.4771	0.2622	0.0248
Electrical equipment	36	0.4255	0.2936	0.0285
Class I motor carriers of general freight		0.1018	0.5890	N.A.
U.S. scheduled airlines		N.A.	0.3827	N.A.
Class I railroads		0.2070	0.4728	0.0928

Note: N.A. = not available.

Similarly, it is difficult to determine how train crews, track and structure maintenance, and other such intercity costs are directly related to specific traffic.

There are great difficulties in determining who "sold" railroad traffic. Was the traffic representative at the origin responsible, or the representative who was working with the consignee at the termination point? Was it the off-line representative or the clerk who received the car order from the shipper? While this problem exists in many transportation selling situations (as well as manufacturing, such as ethical drugs), it is a striking problem for railroad managers.

As suggested by table 6-1, railroads spend a relatively large portion of their revenue for payroll. The ratio of payroll to revenue for most industries is substantially smaller than that of railroads. Certainly, many industries not in this sample may spend equal portions, but the size of the companies in such industries tend to be relatively smaller.

Unlike their manufacturing counterparts operating at similar levels of revenues, railroads spend less on buying materials compared to buying the productive capacity of employees.

This is important in considering the nature of the management task of railroad enterprises. As stated by Kent Healy, "a large share of labor is more decentralized (compared to manufacturers), not working under close supervision within the confines of a building."[3] Also, as orgainzations increase in size, it becomes increasingly difficult to communicate between all relevant parts of the enterprise, a feature that has been observed earlier to be, or perceived by railroaders to be, important. Also, unlike manufacturing where workers may be paced by machines or co-workers, railroad workers are not. And, it is generally considered difficult to reward for high quality, or punish for poor quality, performance when the service is difficult to measure or is produced by a large group of employees.

Table 6-1 also points out the relatively high level of capital expenditures made by railroads to support a dollar of revenue. Because of the relatively low material input, railroads find themselves in a labor-intensive *and* capital-intensive industry.

Certainly these features, as well as those described in chapter 3 illustrate the high degree of similarity of the individual railroads to one another. But in several respects the dissimilarities, generally observed but so frequently not interpreted by railroad managers, represent a rich area of examination. In my research I frequently heard that individual railroads are faced with substantially different situations; thus it is impossible to compare their performances. I agree with the first part of this observation, but not the second. These differences do appear to have contributed directly to the different performances of the railroads I observed. I found several clear patterns of performance with reasonable correlations between the operating conditions, as described by relatively few descriptive variables, and the levels of performance of individual companies. When the companies that make up the railroad industry are arrayed based on these operating characteristics, the patterns of performance raise important questions about whether these conditions are adequately dealt with by the "conventional" organizations and management styles that have been so broadly adopted by the railroad industry.

While there are many means of characterizing railroads and their individual operations, I propose the following as a new approach that contributes a new perspective to understanding the railroad management task. Railroad operations are comprised of a mixture of (1) movements and (2) transactions. By *movement*, I am referring to the physical process that most people would relate to a change in location (usually over a significant distance) of goods (or passengers). This is primarily seen in intercity or road "operations" of a railroad. By *transactions*, I am referring to conducting, recording, and/or performing a piece of business. In the railroad sense, I see the local operations of switching, yard operating, and record keeping, which are generally associated with terminals, as being basically transaction oriented. However, there is some degree of transactions involved in intercity operations. These transactions include handling cars at intermediate yards (between the origin and destination terminals) while enroute. For a variety of operating reasons, this distinction is being reinforced by the efforts of most railroads to avoid enroute rehandling of individual cars at intermediate yards. Where such handling occurs, substantial effort and investment have been expended to streamline the process to minimize the transaction content of intercity movements.

I have found that there is a natural tendency of railroaders to focus on the movement nature of their business. This is hardly surprising since railroads were created to perform movement. Many of the transactional aspects of railroading have evolved because of the development of the complexity and volume of activities of the economy the railroads find themselves attempting to serve. The subtle change over a long period in this demand and its implications have possibly escaped the observation of the railroad managers who have been immersed in the problems of managing the movement features of their companies.

For example, most railroads and their regulator, the ICC, focus on the measures of performance and efficiency that deal with movement: ton miles, miles, train miles, etc. Relatively little attention has been devoted to attempting to measure cost by most railroads or the ICC. As a researcher I was greatly frustrated to find so little data on the volume and nature of transactions conducted by individual railroads. When the data were found in isolated cases, it was often related to specific yards or terminal areas. There was little opportunity to make comparisons between yards or railroads in a macrosense because of the lack of consistency in measurement and incompleteness of the data. While it is not a completely adequate measure of the degree of transactional orientation of a railroad, one crude measure is the average length of haul. Based on the earlier distinctions between movement and transaction content of railroad activities, it might be concluded that railroads with relatively shorter average lengths of haul might be characterized as being more transactional. Of course, this is a crude correlation. One may easily point to short-haul railroads that exclusively operate unit trains and thus substantially minimize transactions, or long-haul railroads that have extensive rehandling of cars enroute at intermediate yards. If I had not been able to observe some trace of patterns in the data, I would have accepted these flaws as possibly masking the influence of the transactions in railroad performance. These possible flaws in the data would have tended to make all railroads appear to be more similar in terms of performance when examined on the basis of length of haul. However, clear distinctions were still evident. Railroads with relatively shorter average length of haul (which I equate to high transactional content) behaved differently than their counterparts with longer average length of haul.

Analysis of Performance of Transaction-oriented Railroads

The data used in the following analyses are taken from or calculated from

Table 6-2
Description of Railroad Performance Measures and Operating Descriptors

CL	Thousands of carloads per year
CL/MI	Thousands of carloads per mile of track in the railroad's system
FREV	Freight revenue, $1,000 per year
FRTD	Freight density, thousands of ton miles of traffic per year per mile of track in the railroad's system
GO	General operating expenses, $1,000 per year
GO/FREV	Ratio of general operating expenses to freight revenue
MI	Miles of main-line track operated in the railroad's system
REV	Total revenue, $1,000 per year
T	Transportation expenses, $1,000 per year
T/FREV	Ratio of transportation expenses to freight revenue (also to be referred to as the transportation ratio in this context)
T/REV	Ratio of transportation expenses to revenue
TGO	Transportation expenses plus general operating expenses, $1,000 per year
TGO/FREV	Ratio of transportation expenses plus general operating expenses to freight revenue

Note: For detailed definitions of variables, refer to *Moody's Transportation Manual* and the *I.C.C. Standard Accounts*.

the ICC reports of major railroads in the United States. A listing of the key descriptors is presented in table 6-2. This table serves as a useful reference for the discussion of statistical analyses that follows.

It may be argued that ICC data are not fully reliable. While I recognized possible deficiencies, the data were useful and satisfactory for my purposes for several reasons: First, the purpose of this analysis was diagnosis of the situation facing railroads. I was not looking for precise calibration of detailed cost structures, but was primarily interested in observing patterns and anomalies in behavior. When I observed patterns that were counterintuitive or appeared to contradict conventional wisdom, I used the finding to point me to where I should focus my field investigations.

Second, the railroads do attempt to follow the prescribed ICC accounting procedure. This does help comparability. The problems of comparison occur primarily in that several of the accounts do include items that companies have a degree of freedom in deferring as expenses. Since expenses can be deferred beyond the year in which they might naturally occur, it is difficult to measure the activity (such as operating trains) and recognize the impact (maintenance of track). For this reason, I focused attention on two accounts: transportation expenses and general operating expenses (which roughly equate to what might be called general and administrative in conventional accounting terminology outside of the railroad industry).

The ratio of transportation expense to revenues is considered by many to be one of the most reliable financial measures of railroad operating performance. Transportation expenses include the field and direct operating labor expenses of operating trains and hauling cars. It reflects what is called the transportation function of the company. It specifically excludes maintenance of the track and structures, maintenance of equipment, and depreciation. There are several advantages to eliminating these last three expense categories. Maintenance of a railroad may be deferred by management for several years in periods in which the cash flow or earnings are depressed. So, within limits, such expenditures may be discretionary in any particular year. Also, different railroads may have different operating practices and preventative maintenance policies that make these figures fairly unreliable. The fact that the transportation cost does not include depreciation is also fortunate because it eliminates the problem of different depreciation policies among railroads and the fact that some railroads are operating very old, previously depreciated equipment.

The issue of which revenue to include in the calculation of the transportation ratio presented a problem. Should it be freight revenue or total rail revenue (the difference primarily being passenger revenues)? In 1960 most railroads still had a recognizable passenger income, while by 1970 freight revenue and total rail revenue were nearly the same. I have followed the practice of focusing on freight revenues. However, when I compare 1960 and 1970 findings, I present both figures for the earlier year.

Prior to my quantitative analysis, I believed that short-haul carriers would have a ratio of transportation expenses to freight revenue (transportation ratio of $T/FREV$) that would be higher than that of carriers with longer average length of haul, provided that the individual carriers in both groups were operating in balance (ratio of carloads terminated to carloads originated ranged between 80 percent and 120 percent). On the average, I found this to be the case. However, the dispersion in the performance of the short-haul (0 to 350 mile average length of haul) carrier group was substantial, while the long-haul carriers were relatively consistent. Why? Regressing the transportation ratio with other descriptors of railroads suggested several avenues to explore. There was striking correlation ($R^2 = 0.839$) between the transportation ratio and the number of carloads handled per year, and a weak relationship ($R^2 = 0.078$) between the transportation ratio and the freight density.

The relationship of the transportation ratio of short-haul railroads and the miles of track in the 1970 data was:

$$T/FREV = 0.3414 + 0.00001336\ MI \quad (R^2 = 0.904)$$

Where $T/FREV$ = Transportation expenses to freight ratio

MI = Miles of main-line track operated in the company system

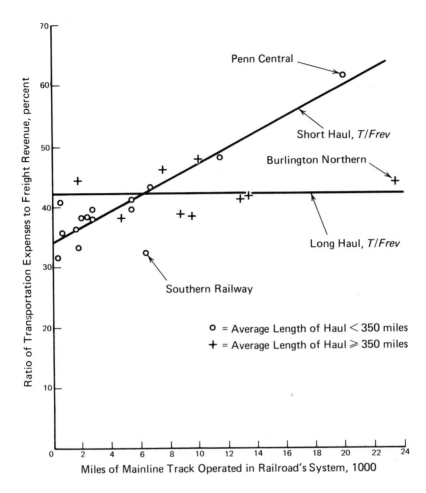

Figure 6-1. Transportation Ratio vs. Main-Line Miles Operated, 1970

These data are also presented graphically in figure 6-1. In this figure, several points deserve special attention. First, the selection of 350 miles average length of haul as the cut point requires an explanation. As the data were processed, several cut points were tried. Cut points below 350 miles produced essentially the same coefficients of regression but with slightly reduced correlation measures (lower R^2). Higher cut points yielded reduced coefficients of regressions and reduced correlation measures. Therefore, the 350 miles cut point was arrived at in a rather mechanistic fashion. Second, a test was made to determine if there was any consistent correlation of a mix of interline to on-line traffic with the transportation ratio. There was no evidence that this was a significant factor. Third, two specific data points are striking in figure 6-1. One is the point from the

Penn Central because of the large scale of its operation for a relatively short-haul railroad. In this case, the most difficult combination of characteristics to manage, one might well expect poor performance, as figure 6-1 confirms. The other point is the Southern Railway. Its performance is substantially better than its average length of haul and scale would suggest. This inconsistency of performance led me to a closer examination of the Southern Railway, which is discussed in detail in chapter 8. At this point, I will simply note that the Southern Railway has developed styles of operation and management that are substantially different from most other railroads in the same category of average length of haul and scale.

Transportation ratio ($T/FREV$) was examined as a function of miles of track (MI) for the same average length of haul for the 1960 data. The results were:

$$T/FREV = 0.3952 + 0.00001228\ MI \quad (R^2 = 0.378)$$

$$T/REV = 0.3617 + 0.000005307\ MI \quad (R^2 = 0.211)$$

Where T/REV = Transportation expenses to total revenue (including passenger)

The results of these analyses are presented as trend lines in figure 6-2 together with the average $T/FREV$ for long-haul railroads. It is remarkable how very similar the results of the two data-base years are. This is particularly striking when it is considered that several significant mergers occurred in the decade that separates the two points in time, and some substantially larger system mileages went into the 1970 base. This suggests that as these systems increased in mileage, the performance deteriorated in a predictable pattern that was suggested by the 1960 data. That is, as the mileage of the system of a short-haul railroad increases, so does the transportation ratio.

It appears that the conventional form of railroad organzation is relatively well suited for long-haul and short-haul railroads, provided the latter do not operate systems much in excess of 8,000 miles. Beyond that point, there is a tendency to lose control of the transportation expenses on short-haul railroads.

It might be argued that this comes about for several reasons. Perhaps the enlarged systems have resulted in more track with lower density, which in turn increases the transportation ratio. This is a meaningful argument, but it appears to be secondary to the really more striking fact that the transportation ratio is heavily influenced by the volume of carloadings (which we suggest is a surrogate for volume of transactions) handled by the railroad.

The analysis of the transportation ratio as a function of density indicat-

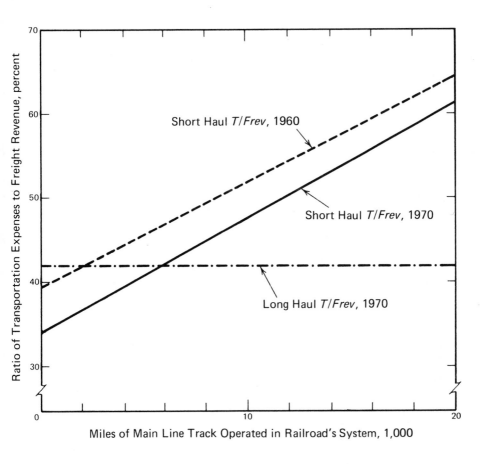

Figure 6-2. Transportation Ratio vs. Main-Line Miles Operated, 1960 and 1970

ed no correlation. When density was added to the mileage variables, a modest increase in correlation occurred for short hauls.

$$T/FREV = 0.3102 + 0.00001276 \quad MI + 0.00000976 \quad FRTD$$

$$(R^2 = 0.9111)$$

While the miles of track operated was one measure of scale and geographic dispersion, I was more interested in the volume of transactions. Does performance deteriorate as volume increases? Which factor is more likely to result in this breakdown of transaction control: (1) increased geographical dispersion of the transactions, or (2) increased volume of the number of transactions? The quantitative analysis suggests that it is a combination of both factors. This can be seen by comparing three equations for the short-haul railroads:

$$T/FREV = 0.3414 + 0.00001336\ MI \quad (R^2 = 0.904)$$

$$T/FREV = 0.3414 + 0.0000434\ CL \quad (R^2 = 0.839)$$

$$T/FREV = 0.3436 - 0.007720\ CL/MI + 0.00004443\ CL \quad (R^2 = 0.857)$$

Where CL/MI = Thousands of carloads per year per mile track in the system

CL = Thousands of carloads per year

As might be expected for this group of short-haul railroads, there was a strong correlation ($R^2 = 0.936$) between carloads per year (CL) and miles in the system (MI), which makes identification of individual influences difficult. It appears that increases in the transportation ratio ($T/FREV$) are related to increases in the volume of transactions; however a reduction in cost is achieved if the geographic dispersion (as described by CL/MI) is reduced. In fact, approximately 3 percent of the regression coefficient of the third equation was provided by the geographic compactness of the transactions (CL/MI), while 97 percent was derived from the volume of carloadings per year.

So, the transportation ratio of the short-haul railroad was highly sensitive to increased number of transactions, and this sensitivity was further increased with increased geographical dispersion.

How does this compare with long-haul railroads (average length of haul greater than 350 miles)? Regression analysis of this group suggested that the transportation ratio did not appear to be related to miles in the system or volume of transactions in direct contradiction with the situation found among the short-haul railroads. However, there was some slight dispersion in the performance of these companies.

The most significant relationship I found for these long-haul railroads was the modest correlation of transportation ratio and freight density.

$$T/FREV = 0.4949 - 0.01948\ FRTD \quad (R^2 = 0.347)$$

Reduced transportation ratios were related to increased traffic density consistent with conventional wisdom.

Thus, for one group, the short-haul transactionally oriented railroad, the ability to control transactions is vital. For these railroads, the problems of control were significantly increased as the volume of transactions (CL) increased, and even more importantly, there was a compound effect when this volume increase was coupled with increases in geographic dispersion.

For the long-haul, movement-oriented railroads, the significance of dispersion and transaction volume was reduced as the nature of the management task shifted to the control of movement cost. Here, the most significant factor in the reduction in transportation ratio was an increase in freight density.

This appears to suggest that there are two substantially different types of railroads that certainly suggest the need for different management orientations and structures for their accomplishment.

The next question is, are the general operating expenses of larger companies significantly lower as a percentage of revenue to offset the increased transportation ratios that might stem from larger, short-haul systems?

General Operating Ratio

I believe that the reported general operating expenses are considerably more subject to management discretion than the transportation expenses. However, I am not willing to disregard them totally. Also, conventional wisdom suggests that they are more or less independent of the size of the railroad or volume of freight hauled. This would mean that the ratio of general expenses to freight revenue ($GO/FREV$) would be expected to decrease with increased volume. This has led many companies (with the general support of the ICC) to attempt such reductions through merger strategies.

After the data are segmented into the short-haul and long-haul categories, as was done in the previous analysis of transportation ratio, the general operating ratio ($GO/FREV$) was related to measures of volume and the log of measures of volume (such as revenue or carloads). For relatively balanced short-haul railroads, the relationship was:

$$GO/FREV = 0.1477 + 0.000005321 \; FREV - 0.01377 \; LOGFREV$$
$$(R^2 = 0.456)$$

Where $GO/FREV$ = Ratio of general and other expenses to freight revenue

       $FREV$ = Freight revenue, \$1,000/year

    $LOGFREV$ = Log of freight revenue, \$1,000/year

For the long-haul railroads, the relationship was:

$$GO/FREV = 0.3064 + 0.0000076 \; 0FREV - 0.03374 \; LOGFREV$$
$$(R^2 = 0.683)$$

There is high colinearity of revenue with other measures of volume, particularly after division of the population by the average length of haul has eliminated a major portion of the distance taper in the rate structure. It would be expected that the number of carloads handled per year might be as good or better a predictor of $GO/FREV$. In fact, it is. For the short-haul railroads, the relationship was:

$$GO/FREV = 0.1788 + 0.00001550\ CL - 0.02046\ LOGCL \quad (R^2 = 0.499)$$

Where $LOGCL =$ Log of 1,000 carloads per year

For the long-haul railroads, the relationship was:

$$GO/FREV = 0.2447 + 0.00002924\ CL - 0.02922\ LOGCL \quad (R^2 = 0.507)$$

It is relatively striking that the regression coefficients of the short-haul and long-haul groups are so similar for the carload descriptors ($1,550 \times 10^{-5}$ compared with 1.924×10^{-5} for CL and -2.046×10^{-2} compared with -2.921×10^{-2} for LOGCL). The primary difference is in the value of the constant (B_0). The long-haul railroads spend a greater portion of their general and administrative ratio that is uninfluenced by the volume of the transactions (24.47 percentage points compared with the 17.88 percentage points of the short-haul railroads). I believe this is related to movement control, but I was unable to secure any reliable correlations with the movement descriptors (such as $FRTD$).

Concentrating on the case of the short-haul carriers, I was curious to determine the level of carloads per year that produced the minimum combination of general and administrative and transportation expenses as a ratio to revenue based on the combination of the models derived above.

$$TGO/FREV = 0.5202 + 0.0000589\ CL - 0.02046\ LOGCL$$

This crude model yields the results shown in figure 6-3. Since it was found that short-haul railroads tended to have values of CL/MI of 0.1 to 0.55, with a mean of 0.25, one might conclude that the optimum level of carloads per year to minimize $TGO/FREV$ might be very low. In fact, there is little evidence that short-haul railroads are particularly successful in offsetting the diseconomy of scale of handling transactions by spreading general and administrative costs over larger volumes of carloadings. If there is any justification for increasing the size of short-haul railroads, it appears that it must come from the spreading of depreciation and the fixed-cost elements of maintenance of way and structure and maintenance of equipment. Or, the justification might rest on the potential of putting together several short-haul railroads to minimize transactions. For example, consider putting together two railroads that each handle 3 million carloads per year. If they normally connect with each other, the result might be one road handling 4 million carloads per year on twice the system mileage. The resulting $TGO/FREV$ would possibly shift to a long-haul pattern

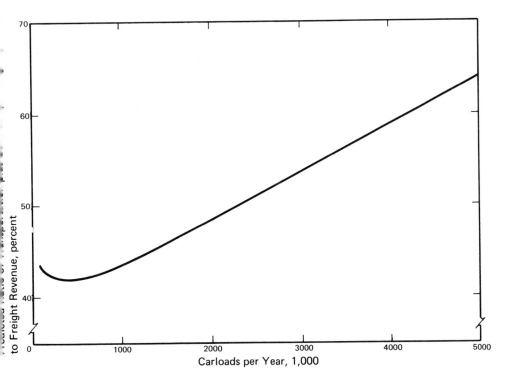

Figure 6-3. Predicted Ratio of Transportation Plus General Operating Expenses for Short Haul (0-350 Miles), Balanced Railroads vs. Carloads Handled per Year

but if it stayed within the short-haul pattern, it is not clear that any improvement in *TGO/FREV* would occur. If the new railroad simply doubled its system mileage and carloads per year, the effect on *TGO/FREV* would be predicted to be disastrous.

Penn Central and Burlington Northern Cases

It is difficult directly to compare 1960 and 1970 performance of *TGO/FREV* because of the shift of mix of passenger and freight business during the interim period. However, table 6-3 presents some comparisons that deserve comment. The table summarizes the data of the Penn Central and the Burlington Northern in 1970 and their predecessor companies in 1960.

Table 6-3

Comparison of Penn Central and Burlington Northern in 1970 with Predecessor Companies in 1960

	Average Length of Haul (Miles)	Carloads Per Year (000's)	System Miles	Carloads Per Year System Mile
Penn Central Case				
1960				
New York Central	242	3,244	10,368	312
Pennsylvania	265	3,713	9,882	376
New Haven	152	635	1,752	362
Total or Weighted Average[a]	245	7,592	22,009	347
1970				
Penn Central	298	5,722[b]	20,467	280
Burlington Northern Case				
1960				
Northern Pacific	461	651	6,800	96
Great Northern	342	1,043	8,292	126
Chicago, Burlington and Quincy	323	1,313	8,659	152
Total or Weighted Average[a]	360	3,007	23,751	131
1970				
Burlington Northern	421	2,560[b]	23,565	109

Source: *Moody's Transportation Manual*, various years.

[a]Weighted on the basis of carloadings.

[b]During the same period, the average weight per carload increased.

In examining the Penn Central, it can be seen that some small degree of increase in the average length of haul occurred from a weighted average of 24 miles in 1960 to 298 miles in 1970. However, the increase was not dramatic and failed to boost the company average length of haul above 350 miles, which would have placed it in the group designated as long-haul railroads. Also, the consolidation did reduce the number of carloads per year from 7.592 million to 5.722 million. However, this is not strictly due to consolidation. In fact, by multiplication of average length of haul by carloads per year, it is seen that the resulting company simply had less carload miles (1.860 million in 1960 compared with 1.705 billion in 1970). Thus, this could not be counted as a measure of the effectiveness of the merger in lengthening the haul or reducing carloadings in a positive way. It might be noted that nothing was gained toward achieving a reduction in the geographical dispersion of the transactions, as measured by CL/MI

(from 347 carloads per year-system mile in 1960 to a disappointing 280 in 1970). Of course, the original intent of the merger did include elimination of substantially more track than was accomplished for several reasons. From figure 6-3 the value of *TGO/FREV* for the Penn Central in 1970 would be predicted to be roughly 0.68. In fact, it was close to this at 0.71. In the period since 1970, the transportation ratio of the Penn Central has shown some improvement. This appears to arise from changes in style of operation since 1970.

The Burlington Northern Case is a different situation. It was the merger of two companies I would categorize as being at the high end of the short-haul group and a third junior partner that was clearly in the long-haul group. The net result was (barely) a long-haul railroad (360 miles weighted average length of haul in 1960 compared with 421 miles in 1970). The amounts of business in 1960 and 1970 were nearly identical at 1.08 billion carload miles. Here the merger lengthened the average haul and reduced carloadings (presumably between companies). While there was little reduction in system miles, or reduced carloads per year-system mile, these factors are relatively less important for controlling *TGO/FREV* in long-haul railroads. One would expect a slight reduction of *TGO/FREV* as a result of this. Recognizing the danger in comparison in 1960 and 1970 figures, we are not surprised to see the 1960 weighted average of *TGO/FREV* drop from 0.53 to 0.53 for the new system in 1970. Of course, 1970 was very early to determine the overall effectiveness of the merger.

Organizational Implications

An organization that decentralizes responsibility and authority is best suited to stimulate greater vigor and finesse in conducting highly decentralized transactions. The performance of the local transactions of the railroad is one group of activities that might be considered for decoupling from the systemic nature of the operation. In fact, this is exactly the way in which motor carriers have coped with growth in their firms.[4] Decentralization is the conventional method of controlling the growth of volume of localized transactions over a geographically dispersed system. But, there are several features of the railroad process that greatly complicate the adoption of such a strategy in this industry today. These issues are discussed in chapter 7.

Effectiveness in Promotion of Integration

It was my belief that there was little integration in the typical railroad organization. I also believed that this could be demonstrated by relatively different attitudes between functions and levels of employees.

Specifically, I set out to test the following hypotheses.

1. Operating, marketing, and administrative (i.e., legal, finance, personnel, etc.) managers had different priorities for action.
2. The greatest functional differences occurred at middle management low levels, and were reduced at top management, vice-president, and higher levels.
3. The operating department was clearly recognized as the most direct line to the presidency, and this recognition provided this functional group a power base from which it could be relatively indifferent to other functions.
4. The operating line managers increased coordination between operations and marketing as relatively low priority, while other managers saw it as a high priority.

To examine these hypotheses I created a very brief questionnaire. Nearly 100 managers from 14 railroads responded.[a] Each respondent indicated his present rank or position, railroad, present role (i.e., staff or line management), and primary functional background (operations, marketing, or administration). Also, each respondent was asked to indicate the most probable functional background of the next president of his railroad and rank order, by importance to his railroad (1 as most important), the following actions: (1) labor productivity, (2) car utilization, (3) speed of local operations, (4) speed of over-the-road operations, (5) coordination between commercial and operating functions, (6) selling, and (7) pricing.

The first point was to determine the power base. What was the functional background that respondents believed would control the presidents' offices? As seen in table 6-4, both line and staff operations managers agreed that operations managers were the most likely, with a minority suggesting administration managers. Marketing was considered a very unlikely background. Among administration managers, administrators were favored over operations managers. Again, the marketing managers were unlikely candidates.

Functional bias was probably operating in both the administrative and operations groups. The responses of the marketing managers was of special interest. While the marketing line managers (mostly in field selling) showed a greater probability of a marketing manager becoming president, it was clear that the operating group realistically had the power.

[a] The following railroads participated in the study: Atchison, Topeka, and Santa Fe; Boston and Maine; Burlington Northern; Chicago and North Western; Baltimore and Ohio; Chesapeake and Ohio; Chicago, Milwaukee, St. Paul and Pacific; Illinois Central Gulf; Kansas City Southern, Louisville and Nashville; Seaboard Coast Line; Southern; Southern Pacific; Union Pacific; and associated railroads.

Table 6-4
Probable Background of Next President of Respondents' Railroads

Background and Role of Respondent	Operations	Administration	Marketing	Total
Operations: Line	63.6	31.8	4.6	100.0
Staff	53.8	38.5	7.7	100.0
Marketing: Line	58.3	25.0	16.7	100.0
Staff	47.1	47.1	5.8	100.0
Administration: Line	0	a	a	a
Staff	36.4	54.5	9.1	100.00

[a]Sample too small to be reliable.

It was reasonably clear that the power rests with operations. Secondary power was found in administration. But, marketing was not perceived as a very direct path to the presidents' offices. Certainly this must influence the thinking of railroad commercial managers.

With this as a background, how do different groups of managers see the priorities for action to improve their railroads? I generally could not find any distinct patterns in the responses of most individual railroads that differentiated them from the whole group. I did find some significant and consistent differences associated with the responses of the managers of the Southern Railway System. For this reason, and because I discuss this railroad in depth in chapter 8, I excluded these responses from the general population. Table 6-5 summarizes the averages of the rankings by functional group and role the various respondents assigned to each action for their own companies. The lower the number, the higher the priority. There are statistical problems associated with averages of rankings. However, the averages presented in table 6-5 give an indication of how different groups assigned priorities. First, line operating managers feel very strongly that labor productivity is a vital area. Of course, this is the primary area of their experience. But it is also largely outside their hands. It is interesting to note that improved car utilization, which is clearly one task of line operations management, was given only average priority by these managers. All functional groups gave improvement in local speed and over-the-road speed mediocre priorities. Interviews suggested two different points working here. There may have been some ambiguity in the question. Increased speed was of little interest to most respondents, but reliability was a concern. Regardless how this point was interpreted by the respondents, product change (for improvement) was not of great interest. There appeared to be substantial satisfaction of the present offering on these two points. The issue of improved coordination is of particular

Table 6-5

Average of Rankings of Importance of Specific Actions Assigned by Line and Staff Managers

| | Respondent's Functional Group | | | | | |
| | Operations Role | | Marketing Role | | Administration Role | |
Action—Improve:	Line	Staff	Line	Staff	Line	Staff
Labor Productivity	1.6	2.1	3.3	2.1	a	3.6
Car Utilization	3.2	2.5	3.5	2.8	a	3.4
Local Speed	5.2	5.0	4.4	5.0	a	5.1
Over-the-Road Speed	5.1	6.4	4.4	5.4	a	6.5
Coordination	4.7	3.6	4.4	2.8	a	1.7
Selling	4.6	4.3	4.0	5.5	a	4.5
Pricing	3.5	4.1	4.0	4.1	a	3.1

[a]Sample too small to be reliable.

interest. First, within any functional group, staff managers place a greater priority on improved coordination than their line counterparts did. As might be expected, the line managers are the backbone of parochialism. Staff managers may be seeing a broader view of the company and find greater need for coordination in their experiences. The relatively high ranking given selling by the line marketing managers, who are primarily in sales management, reflects a tendency toward a functional bias. The attitudes towads pricing are not striking. However, based on interveiws, the high priorities assigned this action by the line operations and staff administration managers come about for substantially different reasons. The former group is simply pushing the blame for problems off on those who establish prices. "If we were to get decent prices, we would have no financial problems." The latter group more typically states that the action to be taken is to develop greater coordination between marketing and operations to become more competitive. One outcome of this would be more competitive pricing.

I offer the following as general observations: The individual functional groups do have clearly different priorities. These differences are diminished to some degree among those in staff roles. But I did not find that staff managers were necessarily seen as important opinion influences among line managers. It appears that railroad staff organizations are promoting integration well. Also, staff managers are quite sensitive to the need for greater coordination. However, there is little sensitivity of this from the operating managers. This is particularly unfortunate since they

Table 6-6

Average of Rankings of Importance of Specific Actions Assigned by Top and Middle Managers

| | Respondent's Functional Group | | | | | |
| | Operations Mgt. Level | | Marketing Mgt. Level | | Administration Mgt. Level | |
Action—Improve:	Top	Middle	Top	Middle	Top	Middle
Labor Productivity	2,2	1.7	1.8	2.8	2.6	3.3
Car Utilization	3.0	3.0	3.8	2.9	3.4	3.5
Local Speed	5.7	5.0	5.3	4.6	5.6	4.4
Over-the-Road Speed	5.8	5.5	5.2	5.0	5.4	6.5
Coordination	4.3	4.3	3.8	3.4	3.3	2.4
Selling	3.7	4.7	4.0	5.3	5.1	4.4
Pricing	3.3	3.8	4.2	4.0	2.6	3.6

also appear to have the power base. They may see cooperation with other functional groups as potentially diminishing this power.

As noted in chapter 5, the top management of railroads may be changing more rapidly in age and orientation than the middle management. How consistent are the attitudes of top managers (vice-president and higher) and middle managers (below vice-president)? Table 6-6 points up some substantial inconsistencies between the views of top and middle managers within the same functional group. It is difficult to find strong relationships between individual groups in table 6-6. But, it may be that the differences between the top managers of marketing and operations are more consistent than between the middle managers of these groups. If this is true, it may be that the functional differentiation flows from the top down, rather than from the bottom up. Rather than seeing the top officers of railroads as the integrators, we see them promoting differentiation, and these values are unfortunatley passed down into the lower levels of management. This would suggest that my second hypothesis was not proven.

Finally, among these respondents who ranked improved coordination as being number 1 or 2 priority on their railroad, how did they rank other actions? Did they agree that there was one specific area to be addressed, or was their concern more defined and systemic? Table 6-7 focuses on these managers who gave improved coordination a first or second place among the seven actions. It would be difficult to say that the responses of this group are significantly different from those of the general population reported in table 6-5. In a sense, this is unfortunate. This group did not point up any unique set of priorities that they would like this improved

Table 6-7

Attitudes of Respondents Ranking Coordination of Operations and Marketing in Their Companies, Priority 1 or 2

Respondent's Function:	*Respondent's Functional Group*		
Action—Improve	*Operations*	*Marketing*	*Administration*
Labor Productivity	2.1	2.8	3.1
Car Utilization	4.0	3.5	3.4
Local Speed	6.3	5.9	5.2
Over-the-Road Speed	5.8	5.3	6.4
Selling	4.3	5.3	4.8
Pricing	3.9	4.2	3.6

coordination to focus on. If improvement comes, it will not be simple. It will probably be a systemwide, integrated change in the way a railroad does its business.

As seen here, the traditional railroad organizations do not appear to promote integration. As I expected, strong functional biases do exist. While there is some evidence of this breaking down among those in staff roles in railroads, it may be that the sources of the biases are top managers themselves, a bad sign for those who are promoting increased functional integration of railroads as a strategy for increased responsiveness to the competitive environment.

Notes

1. John R. Meyer and A.L. Morton, *Improving Railroad Productivity: Final Report of the Task Force on Railroad Productivity* (Washington, D.C.: National Commission on Productivity and the Council of Economic Advisors, 1973), pp. iv-x.

2. See "The Railroad Paradox: A Profitless Boom," *Business Week*, September 8, 1973, pp. 61-63. Also "ICC's Collision Course with Rail Management," *Business Week*, July 6, 1974, p. 7. Also "Railroads: The Prisoners of History," *Transportation and Distribution Management*, May 1971, pp. 24-27.

3. Kent T. Healy, *The Effects of Scale in the Railroad Industry*, (New Haven: Yale University, 1961), pp. 1-45.

4. D. Daryl Wyckoff, *Organizational Formality and Performance in the Motor Carrier Industry* (Lexington, Mass: Lexington Books, D.C. Heath and Company, Inc., 1974), chaps. 4 and 5.

7 Analysis of Alternative Actions

What are the alternative actions (particularly involving modifications of existing organizations) for stimulating management vigor and integration in railroads, and the relative merits of each? This analysis concentrates on the six alternatives suggested in chapter 1.

1. Decentralize the organizations of existing railroads around local profit centers.
2. Reconfigure existing large railroads into smaller railroads that can be effectively managed by existing organizations and managers by breaking up present railroads or separating track ownership and operating companies.
3. Minimize local operating and commercial functions by developing railroads as wholesalers of intercity transportation, abdicating local operations to other institutions.
4. Minimize the need for local management of operating functions by accelerated development of and investment in communications and data processing innovations.
5. Restructure railroad properties to submerge the intense local operations problems of short-haul operations into railroads with predominately more of the easily managed and profitable long-haul operations.
6. Accept existing management organizations and "force" integrative behavior by means other than decentralized profit centers.

Of course, this is only a representative set of alternatives, and they are not necessarily mutually exclusive. Thus, it is quite possible to create a number of combinations of other alternatives from these.

The purpose of this analysis is to judge these alternatives on the following criteria (not listed in order of priority):

1. Potential for promoting integration at levels below the level of the total enterprise
2. Effectiveness in promoting more vigorous and responsive management
3. Capacity for improving cost and service performance
4. Practicality of implementation given the realities of technology; company, human, and financial resources; and traditions.

123

Decentralization Around Localized Profit Centers

In the most extreme form, the alternative of decentralization around localized profit centers is intended to push integrated management decision making and action to the lowest possible level of identifiable geographic operating and marketing units in the company. Such units would desirably be profit centers so that the local manager would become a general manager with responsibility for integrating marketing and operating functions at his unit's level. As such, he would be responsible for generating income, creating local production, and acquiring line-haul production and other services from the system and other local profit centers.

The creation of profit-center accountability would require innovative reporting of a type not presently performed on most railroads. Specifically, income and costs must be identified and associated with the specific profit center. As a model for such a system, I turn to the local profit-center accounting systems that have been adopted by many motor carriers. There are substantial differences between motor carriers and railroads; however, there is probably greater similarity between these industries than between railroads and other types of enterprises. Also, as an industry, the motor carriers are among the most aggressive and effective competitors of railroads. There is evidence that such profit-center systems appear to contribute substantially to the success of the larger members of this related industry.[1]

In these profit-center systems, revenues of a movement are typically divided between the originating and terminating unit (in the motor carrier industry, these are the terminals). There have been several methods devised for the division of the revenues between the origin and destination, but the majority of systems arbitrarily give each half. This gives the terminating unit as much of an incentive to provide service as the originating unit that probably sold the traffic. This provides a partnership bond and mutuality of interest between those at both ends of the traffic lane (or market) pair.

All local expenses are applied against the local unit's share of the revenue division. This leaves the problem of allocating the expenses associated with linkage or movement between the cost-center units. The inter-center expenses (which in the motor carrier industry are essentially the expenses associated with the intercity movement) are usually allocated to the individual local units on the basis of one-half the vehicle miles associated with the traffic that they either originated or terminated. A penalty is assigned for the expenses associated with empty miles generated by imbalanced traffic originated by each unit. This assignment of the intercity or linkage costs may seem to be a relatively arbitrary allocation. While this system may lack some technical elegance, it has the advantage of being simple and consistent. In addition, depending on the proportion of local costs to total costs, the significance of this allocation may be substantially diminished. This is particularly true as the length of haul is reduced.

Besides devising methods of allocating revenues and expenses to geographical subunits, there are two other conditions to be met in establishing such a system. These are control of selling and capital use by the manager of the profit center. If the local unit manager is not in a position to influence the selling situation, he is able to blame failure to achieve profits on the commercial area. In similar fashion, if the local manager is not given authority to increase or reduce the assets he employs, he is restricted in his ability to improve the return on investment of his profit center.

The purpose of such an effort is to devise a means of measuring the performance of the local unit as a business, and the local manager as a general integrative manager to facilitate decentralization. The well-designed profit center is no more than a surrogate for actually dividing the total enterprise into separate, free-standing enterprises, a vital condition for effective decentralization.

The local manager is responsible for integration at a low level and must make the necessary trade-offs between conflicting objectives. Such systems have been described as putting the local manager "in the owner's shoes."

By placing general (or integrative) management at a lower level the decision maker is closer to where the business occurs. The farther one is from the specifics of the business (both geographically and organizationally) the less familiar one is likely to be with the details of the operations and the many subtle trade-offs and opportunities that it is possible to capitalize on.

While such decentralization exposes the integrative managers to a more intimate view of the activities of the firm, it also tends to break up the business into more manageable units that are within the capabilities of lesser managers. This provides the opportunity for the development of general managers at low risk to the company and the individual. At present, on most railroads, the first opportunity to develop experience in such activities is at the executive vice-presidential or presidential levels, which is well past the formative years of career development.

Perhaps one of the most attractive features of this decentralization alternative will be the most difficult to understand by individuals who have been imbued by the bureaucratic values often communicated by the railroad career development process: a vigorous entrepreneurial spirit or the desire to have one's own business. My interviews with railroad managers clearly reflected the present lack of such attitudes in present organizations. Similarly, there was often an expression of a fatalistic attitude of submission among lower and middle-level managers that seemed to stem from the inability to identify directly the impact of contributions of individual efforts. Of course, this feature is greatly amplified if it is reinforced by a system that rewards initiative and actions that promote increased profits such as the profit-center-oriented, incentive bonus programs now adopted by many motor carriers.[2]

In summary, decentralization offers the potential of putting general management closer to where the business occurs, stimulating local initiative, vigor, and entrepreneurial spirit, and the development of general managers. However, this alternative has several serious (and possibly fatal) flaws that must be addressed.

Decentralization implies suboptimization of the performance of individual portions of the enterprise to the possible disadvantage of the overall system. The systemic nature of railroads makes this more than a trivial consideration. However, as a practical matter, I am very suspicious that the highly centralized, functionally differentiated or departmentalized organizations of large railroads may not be achieving optimization because of the enormity of the task, volume of considerations, and remoteness of the central decision makers from the scene of the action.

Besides the issue of suboptimization, there is a question whether a highly decentralized organization made up of individual units concerned primarily with local, day-to-day activities will be capable of sensing changes in the environment and responding to them. However, the present centralized organizations have not received high marks on their performance in this area, and long-range planning is probably best handled by a group that is partially separated from the operating portion of the company. So this is not a serious criticism of that alternative.

If decentralization of the type described here is dependent on a viable profit-center reporting system, then the whole concept depends on the ability to associate revenues and costs with the local unit. Railroad revenues and costs are a complex blend of joint products and costs that are difficult to disaggregate. For a profit-center concept to be viable, the profit-center manager must accept the allocations and believe that the income statement is a fair representation of the situation. Conventional wisdom among railroaders would lead one to doubt that the creation of a profit-center reporting system on a railroad is possible. However, the degree of feasibility of creating acceptable (and hopefully equitable) profit centers is highest among railroads with the shortest lengths of haul (i.e., lower proportion of intercity, joint costs).

Another criticism of decentralization of integration of operating and selling is that the locations where shipper decision-making processes occur (presumably where the selling must take place) and the performance of the operations occur are not necessarily the same. From this, it is argued that because selling and operations are geographically separated, the organizations should be decoupled as well. This situation is particularly true of large multiplant operations, and to the extent that railroads focus their marketing efforts on such shippers, this argument must be considered. However, the use of national account salesmen in a matrix organization relationship with the local managers can substantially offset this situation. An alternative consideration that is even more powerful comes from my study of the most effective intermodal competitors of railroads, the owner-operator truckers. Most of these operators sell their own transportation services and then perform them in a very aggressive way. Rather than decoupling operations and selling geographically, the majority of the commercial activities of these independent truckers are performed within a few feet of the cabs of their trucks.

Another potential penalty paid for decentralization is the cost of redundancy of some services on a local basis that might otherwise be provided from a consolidated facility or group in a centralized organization. An example of this might be the need for decentralized accounting. But, as in the case of accounting, innovative use of communications can permit centralized accounting with rapid turnaround to support local managers without severe cost penalties.

The above are mostly technical problems that are easily recognizable and are far from trivial. But there are greater barriers to implementation of a decentralized profit-center system that stem from institutional factors.

First, for any management information system to be effective, it must be credible to its users. The strength of the belief among railroaders that it is impossible to achieve an equitable allocation of revenues and costs to produce a satisfactory profit-center reporting system is so great that acceptance by managers might not be achieved. Even if the concept were accepted by top managers, it is useless if the concept is not accepted by a vast number of lower and middle-level managers.

Second, the socialization process of management development described in chapter 5 has frightened away potential entrepreneurs and has discouraged the development of entrepreneurial spirit among lower level managers.

Third, most railroad middle managers who might be considered as profit-center managers by virtue of seniority and status seriously lack cross-functional knowledge, experience, or inclination. While the phrase may be demeaning, it is appropriate: "You can't teach old dogs new tricks." Integrative management does demand skills different from the management of functional specialization. As a pragmatist, I consider this to be the greatest single flaw of this alternative, and realistically beyond the capability of the multitude of railroad managers to overcome. The tradition is too old, patterns of behavior are too ingrained, numbers of individuals involved too great, cross-functional experience too insufficient, and management demands too different to be feasible in all but a few isolated railroads.

However, with these discouraging observations aside, it is necessary to note that the Burlington Northern is attempting divisionalization with allocated revenues and costs. At the time of this writing, it is still too early to judge the results of this experiment.

Also, the Canadian National Railroad has established its Grand Trunk lines as separate profit centers. They were partially aided by a clearer means of division of revenues (over the United States-Canadian border) and other considerations. Reports from top management of the Canadian National and Grand Trunk indicate satisfaction with the results and serious consideration of extending the concept to other portions of the system. The Canadian Pacific has taken several steps toward decentralization, but there has not been a movement toward separate profit centers for each portion of the Canadian Pacific Railroad yet.

Reconfiguration

I discuss here two different concepts of reconfiguration: (1) breaking up existing railroads into units of more manageable size, and (2) decoupling track ownership (the predominately fixed-cost portion of railroading) from operating companies, thus reducing the need for large companies to spread fixed costs over a broader base.

The alternative of breaking up the present short-haul railroads into smaller systems is conceptually related to the decentralization alternative described in the previous section. The major difference is that it creates formal, legal entities between the new units (i.e., separate companies) that will probably minimize the opportunities to achieve savings associated with central services. Also, it requires additional transactions between companies in the already Balkanized railroad industry.[3] These additional transactions increase costs and delays, reduce reliability, and increase the transactional problems to be managed.

Such a restructuring would certainly create smaller and more manageable units and would constrict the size of the profit center (even if it is on the level of the firm) since the firms would be smaller.

Besides all of the conceptual arguments against this alternative listed above, there is the fact of the existence of the USRA and Conrail. Rather than break up what some observers described as the most unmanageable railroad in the United States, it is to be enlarged. At this time, the practical matter is that increased integration and management vigor through this form of reconfiguration is a dead issue among these railroads.

The second form of reconfiguration that is possible with unbundling track and operating company ownership may not yet be dead. While the process of unbundling or decoupling the track from the operating companies is difficult to conceive of, its benefits are attractive. For the moment, assume that the federal government could acquire and restore to satisfactory quality a sufficient portion of the track of the American railroads to provide an interstate system. What implications would this have for the structure of the operating companies? What constraints might be relieved, and what innovative railroad configurations might be developed?[4] The concept of federal ownership of the nation's railroad tracks is not new, but what I am considering under this alternative is not simply the old proposition of the passive purchase of the roadbed as a means of creating a capital infusion for sick railroads. Rather, I am looking at the aggressive development of a modern, well-maintained, public railroad track system that would be made available to private carriers, as well as authorized for-hire carriers as alternate routes of convenience. Such a system would mirror the concept of the well-designed, safe, high-speed, super-highway system, and it would be paid for through user taxes.

Presently, substantial portions of the railroad track of the country are in bad order. Whether deferred maintenance, which has led to this situation, was the result of "hard times," excessive regulation, or poor management, the reality is that major parts of the nation's railroad track cannot be operated safely at reasonable speeds. This slow-order track, which places serious limitations on many railroads' ability to provide competitive service, is on their main as well as their secondary lines.

It is relatively easier for railroads to attract capital for rolling stock than for improvement of roadbed. Given the present financial conditions of many railroads that most need track improvement, a lender is wise to demand the security of the pledge of easily retrieved property. The minimum security might be something that the lender can physically take possession of and make alternate use of in case of the failure of the lendee. Rolling stock certainly meets this requirement much better than improvements in roadbed. Thus, because of the conditions of the industry and the nature of the necessary investments, it is questionable whether a prudent private lender would consider track improvement as a reasonable risk at any interest rate without adequate guarantees from the federal government.

There is substantial duplication of trackage over several major traffic lanes that would result in considerable overcapacity if truly productive, high-speed operations were possible.

Privately owned track is a vulnerable sitting target of massive local taxation by every town and county it passes through. It is estimated that $160 million in taxes on right of way are paid annually by the railroads.

This represents approximately 1.5 percent of their total revenue. The situations on individual roads are even more extreme than the average would indicate. For example, the Delaware and Hudson paid ''7 percent of its modest $45 million in revenues for local real estate taxes.''

However, the greatest concern to me in examining the nature of the railroad management task is the massive fixed cost associated with track ownership and maintenance. In many respects, it is the ownership, construction, and maintenance of private rights of way by railroads that make them natural monopolies and drive them towards increasingly larger, but less manageable, enterprises. Once the ownership of the right of way is separated from the operations, it appears that many markets can support several competitors because of the reduced fixed costs. As demonstrated in chapter 6, the best way to reduce the variable costs of a short-haul carrier are to reduce its volume of transactions. The best way to reduce the costs of the long-haul carrier is to increase its freight density. Both are possible once railroading is shifted from a fixed-cost-oriented to a variable-cost-oriented business.

Under this alternative, I propose that the federal government undertake a project to purchase major segments of railroad track and right of way for the purpose of developing a modern, highspeed railroad-track system for public use. This would mean the purchase of some of the existing track and right of way, although that is not mandatory. The railroad would be allowed to continue to own and operate as a private right of way any of its track. Similarly, the federal system would not be obligated to buy undesirable track. The railroads would be responsible for development of classification yards and track connecting their own roads with the federal track system. This feeder track would be analogous with the secondary road that now connects the Federal Interstate Highway System.

Operations on the Public Track System would be in conformance with federal operating regulations. Traffic control through signalling systems would be provided by federal traffic controllers in a role similar to that of the air traffic controllers of the FAA.

Charges for the use of this track system would be made on a user-tax basis, again shifting fixed costs of railroading into variable costs, more like the cost structure of the motor carriers.

As it would be a government-provided facility, it makes sense for several operators to use it jointly. In fact, there are several instances in which railroads are already exchanging trackage rights to each other.

This proposal of nationalization of tracks is certainly preferable to nationalization of railroads, including tracks and operating companies. The federal government has demonstrated greater competence as a developer and provider of facilities than as a manager of operating organizations.

Also, the government has had success in such development projects that were too large an undertaking for any single firm or group of firms in the private sector. The Federal Highway System is a good case in point. One of the greatest criticisms frequently heard is that it has been too successful. Other examples of the skill of the federal government in providing transportation facilities that are then used by firms in the private sector for providing private and for-hire transportation are the federal airways and inland waterways. Other national governments have not proved to be very adequate managers of railroad operations. The foreign railroads operated by national governments that so frequently impress American tourists have not achieved very attractive levels of productivity, and the levels of service that are provided by such railroads are often achieved only through massive subsidies and restrictions on competition from other modes by the governments. This may be for several reasons: First, the governments usually take over failing businesses with substantial social responsibilities. The political manager cannot ignore the claimed social obligations of even the most absurd claim. Second, the governments typically perpetuate old management and conventional railroad organizations. Third, nationalized railroads become employers of last resort. Because of this role, the federal government cannot achieve a normal arm's-length advocate relationship with labor.[5] However, the record of the government acting as cashier for and developer of large transportation facilities has been excellent. Also, the labor relationships in these cases have tended to be relatively stable, perhaps because of the project rather than ongoing orientation of such relationships. I am aware of the Canadian situation, however, and accept the argument that for the two railway systems to maintain some degree of competition for the nationalized industry does reduce the objections listed above.

By creating a public track system, there is the opportunity to salvage the concept of private enterprise in the operation of for-hire transportation. Certainly many railroads do need cash inflow to supply working capital, rolling stock, and improvement of classification and assembly yards. The purchase of some portions of the track to resupply it to the railroads in an improved condition on a pay-as-you-go basis would generate necessary cash flow. This would also secure assets for the government in the event the railroads do eventually fail.

How practical is the concept of federal ownership of railroad tracks? Railroad rights of way are assets that lack a general market appeal. Because of configuration and nature, they hardly make attractive general-purpose real estate. For these reasons, their values are most closely related to their use for railroad track and railroad operations. Some rights of way have been used for highways and transit right of way, but these are fairly isolated situations. Because of the local tax situations that often exist along many rights of way, their ownership may constitute substantial liabilities.

However, it is unlikely that the federal government would take any substantial action until the railroad situation had reached crisis proportions. The political situation would likely have to be a decision between nationalization alternatives. Given the existence of Conrail, there appears to be less chance of such an alternative being implemented unless Conrail were to fail. At that time, the problem of evaluating the value of the rights of way would have to be faced as part of nationalization anyway.

Another reason why this may not be a viable alternative solution at the present time is the resistance from the railroads themselves. While many railroad managers support the concept of federal aid for trackage, they also fear the threat that such participation will include with it the joint-user concept. The Association of American Railroads argues that federal ownership of the tracks:

1. Complicates the problem of optimizing track construction and maintenance standards with equipment design, operating policy, and traffic growth expectations. The result will necessarily be some increase in the overall cost of rail transportation.

2. Presents difficult (although not insurmountable) problems in train control and operations, problems that will necessarily increase the cost associated with the installation and operation of train control systems, to say nothing of the cost of the additional trackwork, which probably will also be involved.

3. Presents special difficulties (*not* readily surmountable) in terminal design and operations, difficulties that will further increase both capital and operating costs.

4. Generally *insures* an increase in the cost of providing railroad fixed plant, because of the intrusion both of politics and of bureaucratic inefficiencies into management decisions.

5. Generally politicizes decisions on:
   a) Fixed plant improvement and maintenance
   b) Abandonment of uneconomic and redundant rail lines
   c) Railroad operating rights
   d) Use of terminals
   e) Grade crossing elimination
   f) Railroad labor contracts, including, most importantly, contracts with operating crafts

6. Opens up the use of railroad fixed plant to private and restricted-commodity carriers, who will enter into rail operations under the guise of

providing ''competition'' for existing common carrier railroad operating companies. These new carriers will skim the cream (heavy, long-haul, base-load traffic) off the railroad common carrier market, all to the direct benefit of the largest industrial corporations.[6]

These operating objections may not be as telling as the Association of American Railroads would suggest. There are certainly those who would argue that opening the railroad fixed plant to competitors would restore *vigorous* railroad competition to the industry. With the separation of the track ownership and operating company ownership, the barriers of entry for the protection of the existing natural monopolies are no longer as justified. So this may only be a disadvantage to the existing business entities that certainly would like to perpetuate themselves.

In many ways this is one of the most conceptually attractive alternatives. But, the political setting precludes it at present. On that basis, it fails.

Minimizing Local Operations

One way to minimize the problem of managing a large volume of transactions is to reduce the volume of transactions rather than to change to better accommodate them. In a sense, this is the reverse of contingency management theory, that is, here we would make the task contingent on the organization. This is not intended as a criticism of the alternative. Given the serious limitations of the other alternatives, limiting or restructuring the operations of railroads is worthy of careful consideration.

The major sources of transactions are in the terminal operations at the origin and destinations, intermediate yards, and interline connections. As discussed in chapter 3, each time a car enters a yard and transactions occur, there is additional cost, delay, error, and potential for missed schedules. At present, there is substantial support for this position among railroaders, even among those who in the past promoted the large automated yards. There is substantial agreement that avoidance of yards (i.e., run-through operations) is highly desirable. Similarly, many railroaders see great advantage in moving cars as large groups (blocks), again to minimize transactions.

However, these steps are already being followed by most railroads. What can be done to further minimize transactions?

If the railroads were permitted to restructure their service offerings to eliminate some terminal functions, substantial reductions in the transactions could be realized. Unfortunately, the area of most likely reduction is reduction of pickup and delivery services, and these are integral to the services the railroads have to offer. So, unless railroads can conceive of new ways to minimize transactions, such as concentrating on line haul (as a wholesaler) and avoiding terminal activities (the retailing), there appears little to be achieved here.

Centralization by Communications and Data Processing

There are at least two approaches to the use of communications and data processing as tools of management relative to centralization of control: The first approach is to use communication technology and the computer to centralize decision making. This substantially diminishes the role of the local field manager to that of inputting information and executing orders. The second approach is to use communication technology and the computer to decentralize decision making. Under this approach, the role of the local field manager is enhanced by the technology. By this, I mean he is supported by better information to make his own decisions rather than to be given decisions.

These two approaches represent substantially different management philosophies and attitudes towards people. The centralization approach partially implies that those at the center are more competent to make decisions than those in the field. In fact, such an approach does have a greater economy of management. Relatively few individuals at the hub of the communications can provide some form of centralized decision making. The rapid improvements in communication technology, such as teleprocessing and electronic data processing, have greatly facilitated such an approach. Also, the "wizard" standing at the hub of the system should be able to understand more fully the systemic implications of decisions.

However, even with the great advances in the technologies that have been made, we still have not reached a point where the central decision maker can observe and assimilate every detail of the multitude of transactions that must occur. So, while central decisions may stress the systemic issues, they fail to provide the finesse of local decisions. Where the system is to produce a highly uniform product of a standard and well-defined specification by a relatively clear-cut process, such detailed finesse is not likely to be a serious consideration. However, this is less frequently true in service industries where customization and attention to the specific details of the service provided are vital. Indeed, the key factors of the most successful service industry firms are: (1) control of the service to conform to the much less clearly defined expectations of the customer, and (2) control of the costs of providing that service. Most railroads are in the service industry, and, in fact, are in one of the most complex segments of the service industry because they provide highly customized services in a multitude of combinations. Based on this position, I am critical of central-

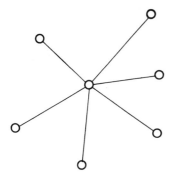 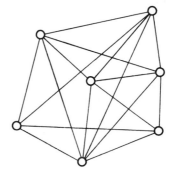

Hub and Spoke Communications   Network Communications

Figure 7-1. Forms of Communication

ized decision making that reduces the finesse and vigor of the adroit local manager. Of course, the nature of the business can be changed to better fit centralized control. One way to do this is to standardize the service substantially and minimize localized variations. The direct way to accomplish this is to minimize local operations and place the emphasis on heavy lanes of intercity unit trains, and other "wholesale" operations. What is interesting about such a proposal is that it greatly diminishes the volume of transactions on the railroad and minimizes the management task in the same way described in the previous section. However, it greatly constricts the market that railroads serve, and this appears to be a dangerous strategy, considering that the railroads' competitors are already quite successfully gaining market shares on a service-competitive basis.

While I wish to promote local aggressiveness, I do not wish to imply that this rejects the use of advanced communications and data processing technologies. In fact, my demands are greater. I stress methods that would allow better coordination between the individual elements of the network rather than simply with the hub, as shown in figure 7-1.

In the network system, some linkages between the parts may be substantially more important than others, while others may not be necessary at all. The one point to be noted is that all parts of the system, as shown in figure 7-1, are connected with the hub. This is because the hub is the repository of data, producer of reports, and score keeper.

The major responsibility of the hub in the network communications system is to provide the members of the system with information on which good decisions may be made.

The problem is that most communications and computer systems that have been designed by (and for) railroads have focused on centralized decisions. Why?

First, this is consistent with a traditional railroad belief that systemic "optimization" was of paramount importance, something that I as an engineer can fully appreciate.

Second, my interviews with railroaders have led me to recognize a pattern of behavior among railroad managers that favors technocratic rather than human-resource-oriented solutions. As the labor force has become more militant there has been more technological opportunity to become less dependent on people. Of course, the labor militancy probably stemmed from earlier introductions of labor eliminating technological innovations described in chapter 3.

Third, some of the early designers of the communications computer combinations were computer technicians who had little railroad-industry operating and marketing experience. So, they were often unaware of the subtleties of the local input. While this is considerably less true now, the patterns of behavior were well established and heavily reinforced by large financial commitments one or more decades ago.

Fourth, there were very mixed reactions among railroad managers about the issue of the role of service as an element of their marketing mix. While most would protest that service is vital, I observed that it took short shrift in many railroad decisions, as discussed in chapter 3.

Fifth, it is simply more difficult to design, operate, maintain, and monitor a communications and computer system that enhances local decision making. Up to this point there have been few hardware and software designers and producers who have been sophisticated enough to handle the task, and there have been too few railroads sophisticated enough to demand it and pay the economic (and emotional) price, commit the management resources, and exercise the discipline to achieve the benefits of such system. The problem may be that the commitments in centralization are so great now that it is too late to change.

Submerging Local Operations Into Long-haul Systems

I compare this alternative to the failing-airline merger strategy that appears to have been followed by the Civil Aeronautics Board, that is, merge failing companies with relatively successful companies. Such practice might be followed in the belief that the management of the successful company will resolve the problems of the failing company. Or, the operation of the successful company, coupled with the failing company, will produce a synergistic effect that will result in a combination more prosperous than the weighted average or sum of the two individual partners.

Unfortunately, the coupling of failing firms with successful firms is often little more than submerging the problem. It may simply be cross-subsidy of one unprofitable business with the income of a more profitable partner, as has unfortunately been the case of several mergers of failing firms with successful firms in the motor carrier and airline industries. An indication of this experience is shown in table 7-1. The cases of motor carrier mergers reported in table 7-1 suggests that the performance of the resulting company quite often most closely resembled that of the weaker of the merger partners. As might be expected, this was clearly the case when the weaker partner was the larger firm. However, it was also often true when the weaker partner was the smaller partner. Another aspect of table 7-1 that has important implications to the railroad considerations at hand are the types of companies being merged. In each case listed in table 7-1, the merger was between a long-haul and regional short-haul carrier. In each case reported here, the resulting companies attempted to maintain full services of the long-haul and short-haul operations. In the cases of several companies listed in table 7-1, the managements elected to focus on long-haul and discourage short-haul business after the time periods shown with substantial improvement in performance.

This action appears on the surface to be a relatively easy step to take, provided ICC or other approval is granted. It has the general appeal of appearing reasonable that successful managers should be able to turn around failing companies. The problems are that failing companies tend to infect successful companies with their illness, the successful companies may be in quite different businesses (i.e., long-haul) and that may be why they are successful. Finally, if the purpose of this course of action is no more than submerging losing operations into successful companies to cross-subsidize them, I would not count this as being a solution. It is a coverup.

Integrative Behavior by Means Other Than Profit Centers

In previous sections of this chapter, I have argued that major changes in present railroad organizations are improbable. This is not so much because they are not desirable, nor is it because many railroad managers themselves do not want them. More than one high-ranking officer of American railroads stated that his greatest desire was to increase the vigor and entrepreneurial spirit of those who worked for and with him. Each of these managers also saw definite advantages of decentralization coupled with local profit centers. However, each also stated his concern that he would be able to develop a set of cost allocations that would be sufficiently credible to his local managers to provide a viable reporting and measurement system. But a more revealing concern was the fear that local managers were incompetent to act, even if they had perfect informa-

Table 7-1
Cases of Mergers of Long-line and Regional Motor Carriers

Merged Carriers	Route Description	Revenues, Year of Merger ($000)	Operating Ratio for Year:										
			1959	1960	1961	1962	1963	1964	1965	1966	1967	1968	1969
Dohrn Transfer	Central	20,679	95.9	98.6	95.0	94.1	94.8	93.4	91.3	91.2	97.4	98.5	98.4
Ramus Truck	Eastern Central	4,410	94.8	96.2	95.1	96.8	97.0	96.4	96.1	99.9			
Hennis Freight	East-South	54,382	96.6	94.1	92.7	91.4	96.4	96.8	95.7	96.1	100.1	97.1	101.4
Red Ball Express	Long-Line Western	4,064	N.A.	N.A.	106.5	99.3	99.2	99.3	96.5	95.6	97.9		
Eastern Express	Eastern	43,420	97.4	103.4	100.8	98.3	98.0	97.8	93.7	95.9	98.6	101.7	97.0
Wheelock Bros.	Long-Line Western	2,386	96.3	97.8	96.3	98.5	107.7	99.0					
Transamerican	Central	52,442	98.4	99.6	99.4	98.0	99.5	98.5	97.9	98.5	103.1	102.0	102.3
Nigro Freight	New England	1,147	98.4	99.9	119.6	97.6	93.0	95.8					
Class I and II Common Motor Carriers of Intercity Freight			95.6	97.9	95.8	95.5	95.8	95.0	94.4	94.8	96.3	94.9	95.7

Source: *Trinc's Blue Book of the Trucking Industry*, Annually.
   Interstate Commerce Commission Annual Report, Annually.

Note: N.A. = not available.

tion in their hands. Their temperaments as described by top managers, were not those of entrepreneurs, and their backgrounds were too narrow to understand fully the range of alternatives they might consider or the implications of their actions if they took them. These concerns among top managers are not trivial, and if they are well founded, and I would have to accept that they are, they will not be easily corrected in the near term. It may condemn the United States railroad industry to having to do the best with what it has, while moving in the direction of greater decentralization very slowly.

For the moment, let us accept this as being the inalterable situation. How can greater integration and vigor be stimulated at all levels of railroad organization while maintaining a high degree of systemic balance and harmony?

Approaching this from a top-down basis, integration must occur among the chief functional officers. This is not an idle comment. In my interviews with railroad managers, I found a high degree of jealousy and antagonism among officers after the initial liturgies stressing team spirit were stated. Similarly, integration tends to occur where the participants (whose functional areas are to be integrated) have approximately equal power bases. This is not true on most United States railroads, and the results of my surveys of railroad managers at all levels indicate that these individuals recognize this as well.

Integration must begin with a top management commitment to balanced power and acceptance of the principle that integration has a value as great as differentiation. Then, this value of integration must be communicated from the individual functional executives downward through their departments. This takes much more than making public utterances to this effect. It must be seen by subordinates in the actions of top management. This means cross-functional support and compromise, and the supporting and rewarding of subordinates who promote integration. This means that the entire company may undertake a direction that more closely approaches matrix management.

This alternative requires a highly flexible and broad-gauge type of junior manager to deal with what may seem to be conflicting objectives, and inconsistent signals (first stressing differentiation along the organizational lines and then encouraging and rewarding integrative behavior). It might be argued that the lower and middle-level manager who is capable of coping with this complex task is probably quite capable of being a successful manager under the decentralization alternative. The company that starts down this path is certainly taking steps that make the alternative much more viable.

The problem is that the development of such lower and middle-level managers requires an investment in training that may be greater than most railroads are prepared to make. Besides the conventional, on-the-job training that so typified the process described in chapter 5, railroads must seek training opportunities that stress broadening rather than narrowing of viewpoints. These might include cross-functional transfers, outside education, and promotion from outside (breaking with the railroad traditions of promoting from within). Finally it may mean paying higher salaries.

A second problem is, can the highly integrative top management team be kept together? A team of managers of this calibre and broad viewpoint is an ideal target for executive searchers looking for chief executives.

Finally, such a system of management is emotional or spiritual, and is held together by the will, energy, and excellence of its leaders. How long such a balance can be maintained is open to question, particularly if the team starts to break up. Perhaps this is an intermediate step toward a more stable form of highly integrative organization.

Notes

1. D. Daryl Wyckoff, *Organizational Formality and Performance in the Motor Carrier Industry* (Lexington, Mass.: Lexington Books, D.C. Heath and Company, 1974), chaps. 4 and 5.

2. Ibid., pp. 40-41.

3. Alexander L. Morton, "Balkanization in the Railroad Industry," *Proceedings of the Transportation Research Forum*, 1974, pp. 14-17.

4. D. Daryl Wyckoff, "Public Tracks, Private Users," *Transportation and Distribution Management*, April 1973, pp. 38-40.

5. Stewart Joy, *The Train That Ran Away* (London: Ian Allan, Ltd., 1973).

6. Association of American Railroads, "Government Ownership of Railroad Fixed Plant," Working Memorandum, 74-10, October 22, 1974, pp. 4-6.

8

Improbable But Successful Solution: The Southern Railway System

It may appear that I have demonstrated little originality in selecting for a detailed case study the Southern Railway, recently described as one of the five best-managed companies in the United States.[1] The *Dun's Review* selection of the Southern Railway for this distinction and my decision to focus on this company to illustrate my conclusions were mutually independent decisions. As shown in this chapter, the present success of the Southern Railway is partially the outcome of essentially two different strategies adopted over a period of roughly 15 years, and some unpredicted, fortunate outcomes.

The selection of the Southern Railway System for this detailed case analysis is not meant to endorse the actions of management or to suggest that all aspects of the company are ideally managed. After studying several firms, I decided on the Southern Railway because it would serve as a particularly efficient case to illustrate several points. My understanding of the situation at the Southern Railway System was greatly enhanced by the number of hours spent with other railroads confirming similarities and dissimilarities.

Also, the following interpretations of the development of the present Southern Railway System's management style, orqanization, and decision-making process are not intended as an official Southern Railway management-authorized history. While the management of the company was very helpful in and supportive of my research, the following should not be considered anything other than my personal observations.

Background

The Southern Railway System (SRS)[a] has experienced excellent growth in traffic, revenues, net income, and return on investment in recent years (see figures 8-1 through 8-3 and table 8-1). For the purpose of this analy-

[a] The term Southern Railway System as used in this chapter refers to the Southern Railway Company and its consolidated railroad companies. It is the practice of the Southern Railway System to consolidate subsidiaries where 50 percent or more of the voting stock is owned. Investments in other companies are carried at cost. Also, unless otherwise stated, financial data reported for the Southern Railway System in this chapter is based on generally accepted accounting principles (GAAP).

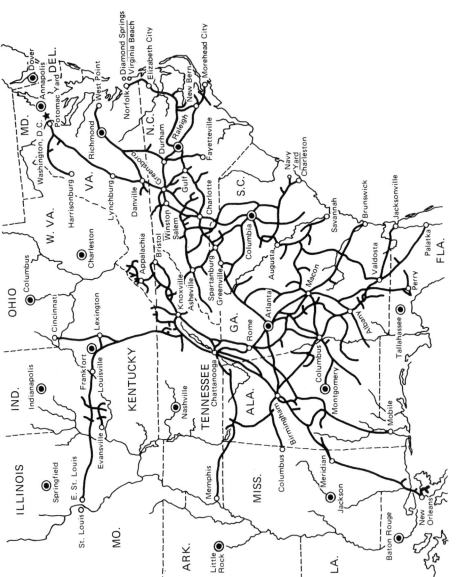

Figure 8-1. The Southern Railway System, Route Map

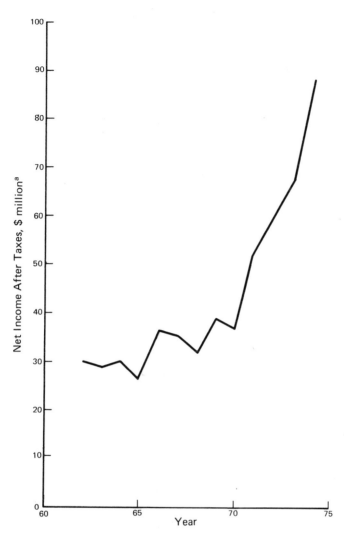

[a]Based on generally accepted accounting practices rather than ICC accounting.

Figure 8-2. Southern Railway System, Net Income After Taxes, 1962-74

sis, I focus my attention on two periods: the years up to and the years after 1967. The year 1967 is an important milestone in the development of the SRS because it not only represents the end of the tenure of D.W. Brosnan as president and the entry of W.G. Claytor, Jr., but it also was the pivotal period in the change of strategy, management style, and organization at SRS. A comment that is often made about the SRS by outside observers is that a major portion of its success may be attributed to the

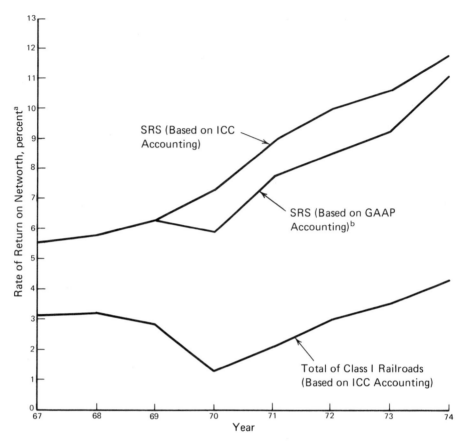

^aCurrent year net ordinary income as a percent of shareholder's equity at beginning of the year.
^bSRS GAAP data not reported prior to 1969.

Figure 8-3. Southern Railway System, Rate of Return on Net Worth, 1967-74

fact that it operates in the rapidly growing market of the southeastern United States. The general growth of traffic of railroads in the Southern District has been impressive (see figure 8-4). However, it appears unreasonable to ignore the fact that the SRS itself has contributed significantly to this growth. As can be seen, the Southern Railway Company had a rate of growth that was notably faster than the entire district (including the Southern Railway Company and other subsidiaries that make up the SRS). Certainly the SRS contributed to the growth of the South, and the

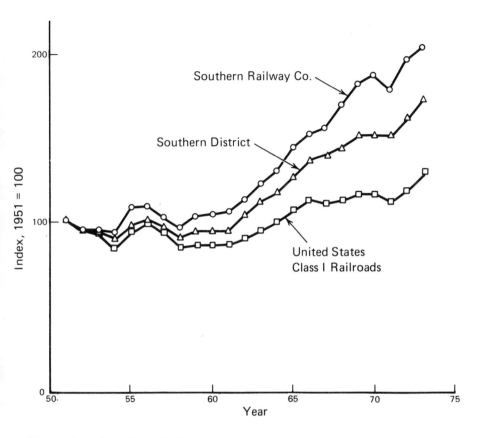

Figure 8-4. Southern Railway Company Revenue Ton Mile Growth, 1951-73 (Index 1951 = 100)

SRS has grown more rapidly than other southern railroads. The reasons for this success go beyond the "fortunate" location of the SRS.

Southern Railway System Prior to 1967

The 1950s saw the SRS undertaking a highly innovative strategy in the operations of the company. In 1953 the SRS was the first major railroad in the United States to convert fully to diesel locomotives. Under the direction of D.W. Brosnan as vice-president of operations, executive vice-president, then president, the SRS appeared to be obsessed with technological innovations and labor-saving automation. This focus on technology and automation was the manifestation of D.W. Brosnan's concern

Table 8-1
Southern Railway System, Summary of Performance, 1965-67

Item	1965	1966	1967
Freight revenues ($000)	412,736	436,028	438,326
Operating revenues ($000)	453,361	474,593	469,843
Tons of freight (000)	115,728	122,968	127,903
Revenue ton miles (million)	30,667	33,460	34,238
Revenue per ton mile, cents	1.346	1.303	1.280
Revenue per car mile, cents	57.2	57.7	58.0
Operating ratio, percent[a]	74.7	70.6	72.1
Maintenance ratio, percent[a]	32.2	30.2	30.8
Transportation ratio, percent[a]	33.4	32.5	32.9

[a]Ratio of expense item to operating revenue.

about the excessive labor content of railroading. He saw two trends that greatly distressed him: (1) increasing labor rates, and (2) increasing militancy and constraints in freedom to operate to use labor in the most effective manner. His objective was to reduce manual effort and dependency on labor through the earliest possible introduction of automation.

This led to several actions. Principal among these were yard investment and changes in yard operations. D.W. Brosnan believed that automated yards should be given the highest priority of any investments on the SRS. Like many other creative and innovative railroad operators of this period, he looked to the automated yard to offer great potential for improved efficiency and reduced labor cost in this vital, but rapidly deteriorating aspect of railroading. Faced with constrained capital resources, he elected to attack this area first. So while automated yards were being built in the early 1960s, there was evidence of irregular investment in the maintenance (equipment and way and structures) area. The first automated yards came into operation in Birmingham, Knoxville, Chattanooga, and Atlanta in the late 1940s and the 1950s. A major automated yard was completed in Macon in 1965.

As this phase of the Brosnan strategy of streamlined operations was being implemented, he turned to upgrading the equipment, then track and structures. His approach to equipment was two-pronged:

First, he observed that most maintenance operations were essentially "custom job shops." The equipment maintenance programs were primarily ad hoc. He was impressed by the practices of the production lines of manufacturers. He studied the automobile industry, and hired an industrial engineer from General Motors to develop a production-line approach to railroad equipment maintenance. Brosnan's first steps in the direction of equipment maintenance occurred at the time that the SRS dieselized. All round houses and steam-locomotive shops were closed and new shops specializing in diesel operations took their place. This meant that a substantially different method of maintenance could be introduced. It was not simply adapting steam-locomotive technology to the diesel. By the end of the Brosnan tenure, basic industrial engineering had been applied to equipment repair and production-line methods had been adopted in every maintenance facility.

Second, Brosnan was convinced that there were great opportunities if a railroad were to approach car design in a radically new way. He was looking for methods of construction that would minimize the ratio of unloaded weight to gross weight of the car to (1) minimize wasted horsepower and (2) maximize carrying capacity for shippers. This led to highly innovative designs and the development of several car designs and new sources. One example of this was the large-capacity, covered hopper car, the " Big John," which is described in a later section. The improved maintenance operation also implied different design criteria and the opportunity to operate equipment that had previously been considered nonmaintainable.

In the area of track maintenance and upgrading, Brosnan had innovative approaches as well. He was successful in promoting the upgrading of the tracks between Cincinnati and Chattanooga (see figure 8-3) in a very creative fashion. The SRS convinced the owner of this track, the city of Cincinnati, to expand its investment in the upgrading project. Today this excellent facility provides a major traffic link for the SRS.

While D.W. Brosnan was innovating in the area of production-line methods of equipment maintenance, he was also actively attempting substantially to automate track-maintenance operations.

Perhaps one of the most interesting points to note about Brosnan's changes in operations has to do with his use of yards. As was mentioned earlier, the SRS was investing substantial sums in automated yards. However, this was also done by some other railroads at the same time and since. But, even with these automated yards, Brosnan established several policies that some other railroads failed to do or to enforce. First, the number of yards a car was handled in was to be minimized, even if the yards were automated. With each handling, there was some cost, even if minimized by automation. But, more importantly, if the yard could be avoided, it would reduce congestion, confusion, and possible errors. Second, cars were to be classified and blocked internally (well within the railroad rather than at major terminating points or connecting gateways). This relieved the pressure on the points, which normally become heavily congested. Third, cars were to be blocked at the earliest point possible.

The innovative actions of D.W. Brosnan in the operating area put the railroad into an excellent position for the next phase of its development. By the time that he left as president in 1967, the operating performance of the SRS was rapidly improving and might be considered excellent by most measures and industry standards.

By 1966, the last full year of the Brosnan era, the compensation (excluding taxes and benefits) paid on the SRS was down to 33.0 percent of operating revenues, compared with 45.8 percent for the total of Class I railroads for the same year. The transportation ratio of the SRS was down to 32.5 percent compared with 38.9 percent for the total of Class I railroads. For the company, only 32.3 percent of the total maintenance of way and structure expenses was paid out for labor, while 55.8 percent was being spent for materials (the remaining 11.9 percent being depreciation). On most other railroads, the proportion of labor was more typically the opposite. Similarly, the labor costs of maintenance per locomotive mile and car mile were substantially lower than other railroads. The innovations of D.W. Brosnan were already having considerable impact by 1967. But even more significant was the timing of their adoption. By innovating early, major capital investments were made before the railroad had been weakened by financial drains and the cost of the investments had inflated. The cost of similar investments in the next decade were considerably higher. Also, by innovating early the SRS was able to eliminate redundant labor before the unions were fully organized to maintain jobs. In most cases, the SRS was able to maximize the benefit of automation and technology, which other railroads were unable to do a few years later.

Marketing and Commercial

The focus of the SRS in the early Brosnan era was clearly directed to the operating aspects of the company. D.W. Brosnan was first and foremost an operating manager. The SRS, like most railroads had a tradition of domination by the operating departments. Marketing in the early periods of the Brosnan era was essentially nonexistent in the SRS. Selling might be characterized as being undirected. While the operations were definitely improving, the growth in traffic and revenues was nominal. It was as if Brosnan believed that the excellence of the SRS operations would be sufficient to attract traffic. The failure of this approach greatly frustrated Brosnan when he became executive vice president in 1960. With the energy and vigor he applied to improving the operations of the SRS, he turned to marketing. His first attempt in this direction could hardly be dignified as a marketing effort. He assembled a group of individuals from the SRS to analyze service performance and reliability. Meanwhile, Brosnan visited and studied the marketing organizations of several major industrial manufacturers. While Brosnan was open to hiring from the outside to supplement SRS personnel in his initial efforts in creating a marketing organization, most of the group was drawn from the operating departments.

He found that the managers on the SRS did not know which parts of the business were contributing to profits. Similarly, there were few measures of quality or reliability of the services, and what the shipper expectations or desires were.

Also, Brosnan believed that there were opportunities to capitalize on the low costs of the SRS operations with rate reductions in some cases. Through selective rate reductions he hoped to prevent further diversion of traffic to the aggressive trucking industry in the South. He found himself very frustrated in this effort. The most publicized example of this was the SRS program to introduce the "Big John," a large-capacity, covered hopper car designed to transport grain at reduced costs.[b]

In the late 1950s the SRS traffic analysis group began to investigate the entire grain industry in the southeastern United States. The analysis showed that while barge and truck traffic in grain had increased at a substantial rate, rail traffic had grown at a much slower rate. The traffic analysis group, comprised primarily of individuals with operating backgrounds and orientation, began to design a light-weight, "bare-bones," 100-ton, aluminum-covered hopper car to compete with barges. SRS proposed to offer rates developed on the basis of average costs experienced on existing grain operations, adjusted to reflect the savings expected from the Big John equipment.

The Big John effort was part of a broader scheme by the SRS to participate more fully in the poultry and livestock-feeding industry in the South, the primary purpose of the grain movement to the Southeast.

As research continued, the SRS analysts found that their earlier focus on the barge competitors was perhaps misdirected. Truckers, mostly owner-operators, who carried truckloads of goods north, were carrying grain south as back-hauls. These truck movements were not regulated by the ICC (under the agricultural exemptions), so trucking rates (not filed) were subject to frequent change. However, the ICC did regulate the rail movement of grain and the probability of a railroad being permitted to introduce innovative rates was considered to be low.

Before movements could commence, the ICC suspended the new SRS rates pending a hearing that began in January and ended in August 1962. At that point, the ICC approved the rates. However, in April 1963 the full commission reopened the proceeding for reconsideration. On July 1, 1963 the full commission reversed the essential findings of the August 1962 ap-

---

[b] For a detailed discussion of the "Big John" case, see Joel D. Goldhar, *The Southern Railway System: Estimating the Potential Traffic Volume for a New Transportation Service* (Boston, Mass.: Harvard Business School, 1965).

proval. In this review, the full commission found the proposed rates had not been shown to be "just and reasonable" and were unlawful.

The ICC actions have generally been interpreted as an attempt to protect the balance of intermodal competition. The suspension of the reduced rates from the SRS was clearly an attempt to maintain the status quo in the competitive balance by frustrating the potential gains that might be realized by technological and operating innovation.

On September 10, 1965 the ICC, after the courts reversed the ICC on appeal, reconsidered its prior decision and substantially upheld the earlier decision and allowed the SRS reduced rates to stand. The SRS had successfully argued that the new rates were sufficiently above anticipated costs to provide a reasonable return. Also, a substantial and growing portion of the grain traffic was being handled by nonregulated truck carriers, and adoption of the new rates would result in substantial stimulation of primary demand for grain shipments into the Southeast.

The series of events pertaining to the Big John grain case had several important impacts that went beyond the obvious anticipated increase in grain traffic on the SRS.

During the Big John case, the SRS assembled a group of individuals who became exceedingly skilled in market research. For the first time, the SRS railroaders found it necessary to go beyond operations and simple freight solicitation. While the ICC could be criticized for placing one barrier after another in the way of the SRS, it was coincidentally stimulating the important development of a new function. Also, as the SRS was preparing the Big John arguments, the company began to gain a much deeper understanding of the entire poultry and livestock industry. The SRS interest broadened from strictly retaining (or gaining) a market share in a competitive situation to stimulating primary demand by taking an active role in the agribusiness of the area it served. The railroad shifted from a passive role to aggressive and active participation in the local economy. In this process, the SRS found itself placing the marketing function in an increasingly more prominent role. This was the first step toward the formation of a true marketing function.

Also, the Big John case appears to have developed a degree of confidence in SRS management in dealing with the ICC. The final settlement of the Big John was not an easy victory. But, the SRS found that it was possible to take on the regulators and win. The spirited attitude of independence of the SRS toward the ICC no doubt evolved from the experience.

While the Big John case was particularly significant, it does not imply that this was an isolated event. A series of less-publicized innovative services and rates were being developed by the end of the Brosnan era in 1967.

A substantial portion of the development of market research and resulting programs were directly under the direction of R.S. Hamilton. His selection by Brosnan to lead the marketing effort raises several questions. Hamilton was the industrial engineer Brosnan hired from General Motors to bring production-line methods to the maintenance operation. After successfully implementing this program, Hamilton spent a brief term at the New York Central in similar activities. But Brosnan wanted to bring Hamilton back to the SRS for traffic analysis that was to develop into a full marketing program. Brosnan's selection was not based on Hamilton's previous experience in marketing or research. However, Brosnan appears to have had considerable confidence in Hamilton's ability to adapt. Also, Hamilton had operating credibility. This was vital to Brosnan, given the operating orientation of the SRS in the 1950s. In many respects, the marketing activity was a natural extension of the operations of the SRS at this point. It is interesting to note that Brosnan raised the compensation level of Hamilton to a level above that of the head of operations for a period of time. Brosnan clearly set the pattern for the development of a true marketing function at the SRS.

Organization and Management Style

D.W. Brosnan has been described as an autocratic, authoritarian, "one-man band." He appeared to have had little patience for those who worked with him and for him. He was considered by operating managers at the SRS and other railroads as an outstanding and innovative developer of railroad operations. However, many of his managers were terrified by him and his abrupt and heavy-handed demands. He preferred to make most decisions of any consequence personally, and he frequently failed to take the time to communicate his strategy or reasons for these decisions to others. This personal management style often left upper and middle management puzzled as to what actions to take. Such a style of management did little to develop the managers who worked for him. However, his personal charisma and dictatorial demands developed a high respect of authority in the SRS organization. This was to have important implications later.

To understand the events leading to 1967, it is necesary to understand Brosnan. He was first and foremost an operating manager. His strategy was to focus on individual features of the railroad, in turn: the modernization of the locomotive fleet, industrialization of equipment maintenance, and automation of track maintenance and construction. He believed that he would attract traffic with the implementation of this strategy that would result in a streamlined and highly efficient railroad with minimum dependence on labor. His strategy increased traffic by virtue of his personal energy and authority and accomplished all that he had hoped for except the key element. His strategy adjustment of creating a marketing arm was a major step toward correcting this failing, but his inability to recognize the imbalance in the operating-marketing power base seriously limited its overall effectiveness. Also, his inability to delegate authority, develop managers, and maintain organizational and self-discipline (compared to authoritarian rule) had reduced his effectiveness as a manager by 1967. D.W. Brosnan set the direction of the SRS by his strategies; the railroad had taken the steps to achieve operating excellence and efficiency. In fact, most of the executives who led the SRS in its next phase were selected and trained by Brosnan. The next phase was to capitalize on this. It became increasingly apparent that the railroad was on the threshold of a new era that demanded a new strategy and a new chief executive.

Southern Railway System After 1967

When W.G. Claytor, Jr. assumed the presidency of the SRS his primary task was to capitalize on the efficient operations that had been developed during the Brosnan era. Claytor, a lawyer with no railroad operating or marketing experience, entered a company with highly motivated and competent managers. But, as in most railroads, the operations organization was the dominant functional group. Managers had a positive attitude toward what could be accomplished, but the company had long operated in an authoritarian, unstructured, and unevenly disciplined mode.

Claytor's first task was to resolve a number of labor problems that had been generated in the closing years of the Brosnan tenure. For this task, he relied heavily on George S. Paul, who rejoined the SRS in 1968, having left the company in 1967. Later, Paul became the executive vice-president of administration. In this role he was to have an important part in developing the committees that managed the SRS. Claytor then turned to the task of capturing the potential benefits of the tentative and struggling efforts of the SRS in building a marketing function.

Claytor was not aligned with any functional group by background or previous experiences. He felt strongly that a balance of power and influence between the operation and commercial functions had to be created. Also, because of his lack of experience and detailed knowledge of the technicalities of the functional areas, he was forced to delegate rather than dictate. Under Claytor, a novel form of management evolved in the SRS. While the formal organization chart of the SRS generally resembles that of traditional railroad organizations (figure 8-5), the manner in which SRS management operates is highly unusual. As the result of skill and energy, forceful discipline, and historical accidents, the top management of the Southern Railway System achieved excellent results with a traditional

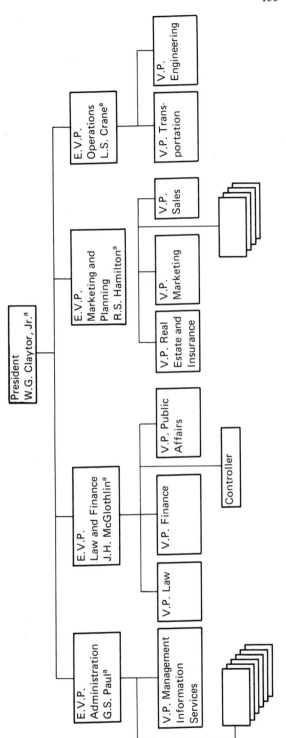

^aMember of Management Committee.

Figure 8-5. Southern Railway Company, Abbreviated Organization Chart, 1974

Table 8-2
Southern Railway System, Summary of Performance, 1968-74

Item	1968	1969	1970	1971	1972	1973	1974
Freight revenues ($000)	478,912	536,887	571,983	620,712	698,635	747,954	871,995
Operating revenues ($000)	517,579	586,567	602,573	647,405	723,798	778,745	909,325
Tons of freight (000)	133,604	139,179	140,297	134,302	147,959	149,397	153,189
Revenue ton miles (million)	37,320	40,172	40,740	39,847	43,869	46,144	47,955
Revenue per ton mile, cents	1.307	1.336	1.404	1.558	1.593	1.621	1.818
Revenue per car mile, cents	60.0	62.6	68.3	75.6	78.8	80.9	94.1
Operating ratio, percent[a]	71.0	71.8	72.3	71.6	70.3	71.7	72.6
Maintenance ratio, percent[a]	31.6	32.6	33.9	35.4	34.2	34.1	34.7
Transportation ratio, percent[a]	31.7	31.5	30.8	29.2	29.5	30.9	31.4

[a]Ratio of expense item to operating revenues.

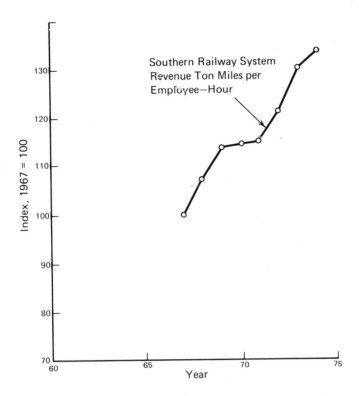

Figure 8-6. Southern Railway System, Labor Productivity per Employ-
ee-Hour, 1967-74

railroad organization structure (see table 8-2). These results of the SRS
are directly related to the substantial vigor and high levels of integration
and coordination of operations and commercial functions at all levels of
the organization. At the heart of this mode of operations is the SRS management committee.

Operations

The operations of the SRS after 1967 might be characterized as a natural
extension of the previous period, (after 1970 directed by L. Stanley
Crane, trained by Brosnan). The strong influence of D.W. Brosnan continued to be seen in operations. A major automated yard was built in 1974
at Sheffield, Ala. Innovative car designs continued, and production-line
equipment maintenance and highly automated maintenance of way were
further refined. Labor productivity increased, as seen in figure 8-6. The
cost of transportation was tightly controlled to the point that the SRS was

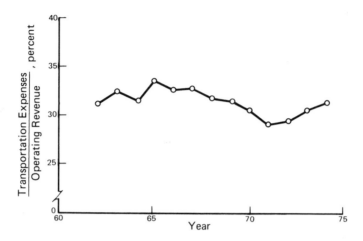

Figure 8-7. Southern Railway System, Transportation Ratio, 1962-74

able to make selective rate reductions or refuse rate increases, while maintaining an essentially level transportation ratio as shown in figure 8-7.

The SRS began to realize substantial benefits from the operating improvements and investments made in the Brosnan period. The practice of minimizing use of yards, high-speed automated yards, and internal blocking facilitated the economic viability of operating shorter trains. As seen in figure 8-8, as the trains were shortened (indicated by reduced revenue tons per train), the increased speed of the trains substantially increased the ton miles per train hour. Also, the impact of investment in new, large-capacity cars is seen as an increase in revenue tons per loaded car in figure 8-8.

The SRS operation was a delicate balance between centralized and decentralized control. As dieselization occurred, locomotives were no longer specifically assigned to divisions. Centralized control of road locomotives and cabooses were the first step in reducing the traditional autonomy of the division superintendent. It was intended that other activities, particularly car control, also be centralized. However, this intention was frustrated.

The attitudes of the Brosnan period toward authority had important impacts in the post-Brosnan period. While Brosnan was authoritarian and dictatorial, he was not always disciplined. Local management was able to maintain greater autonomy than might have been possible otherwise. The pattern of management that beqan to evolve was not particularly recognized by most individuals at the time and is still not fully understood by

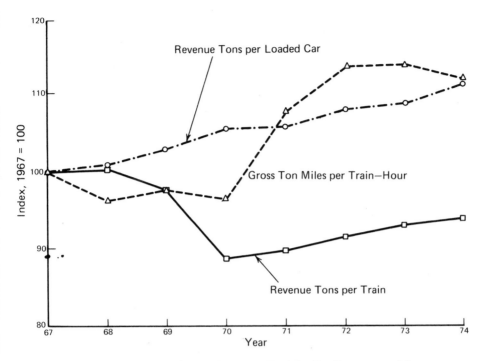

Figure 8-8. Southern Railway System, Freight Performance: Measures, 1967-74

some SRS managers. While management talked of centralization, steps were being taken that amounted to a remarkable degree of de facto decentralization. Better information was being made available to the field to make local decisions. Policies rather than orders were being transmitted to the field. While policy making and system coordination were highly centralized, execution, within these policies, was still autonomous (relative to what was occurring on other railroads). One example of this is the comparison of the car control and inventory systems of the SRS and the Southern Pacific Transportation Company in chapter 3. In a sense, had Brosnan been more able to force greater discipline by more delegation in the conventional sense, the vigor of local management might have been sapped as it was on other railroads. Today, the local field managers have a relatively high degree of freedom to act. Substantial changes by field managers can be made and are. The primary condition is that these changes must be coordinated with the center.

Another aspect of the SRS that characterized the operation was the philosophy that there was no necessity to compromise service to reduce cost. Whether this assumption was correct or not, the basic belief that it was true was apparent in several interviews with operating managers. They stated that they believed it may not cost more to provide fast and reliable service. This operating premise appears to be based on a Brosnan philosophy that the longer a car takes to perform a service, the greater the cost will be. While there may be some detailed technical arguments whether this is always a valid statement, belief in it creates a very positive pattern of behavior that is very consistent with a marketing orientation.

The SRS had developed an agreed-upon methodology for determining the contribution specific traffic and operations made to profits. Since it is highly confidential, it is difficult to know how sophisticated it is. However, it appeared to be fairly effective. First, managers were decisive and acted as if it were "true." While it may not have given correct information in every case, at least the SRS managers were decisive and were guilty of errors of commission rather than paralysis. Second, the methodology was correct enough to be producing a satisfactory, if not perfect, model of the costs.

The SRS devoted a substantial effort to monitoring train performance. As this occurred, the company began to develop a substantial data base to be used in simulations of alternative train operations. This eventually led to the ability to simulate specific changes, such as the addition of individual trains, and to be able to predict resulting speeds, fuel consumption, reliability, and other features of the operations.

In the post-1967 period, the SRS found that it was in an earnings position to start major investments in car and track maintenance. First, earnings were increasing, and tax incentives provided a good inducement to reinvest in improving the physical plant. Second, the SRS innovations in automated maintenance of way equipment and practices gave the railroad maximum leverage. As seen from figure 8-9, the evidence was that the SRS was banking maintenance, that is, investing pretax earnings in upgrading the facilities of the railroad in good years. In years in which operating expenses excluding maintenance are a high percentage of revenue, maintenance expenditures were minimized. This is not an unusual railroad practice, as described in chapter 3. However, since 1967 the SRS appears to have had the discipline to make such investments or expenditures in good years.

Marketing

The marketing efforts of the SRS of the type that were symbolized by the Big John case of the earlier 1960s set the thrust of this group after 1967. The task was to determine what traffic was desired by the SRS, the costs to provide the services, and what it would take to keep or obtain the busi-

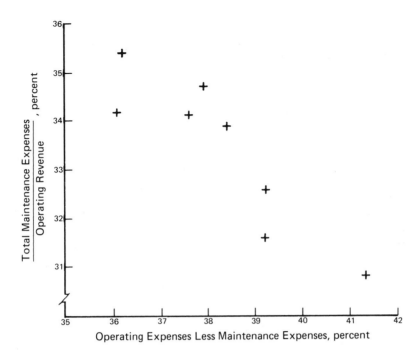

Figure 8-9. Southern Railway System, Total Maintenance Expenses per Operating Revenue vs. Operating Expenses Less Maintenance Expenses per Operating Revenue, 1967-74

ness. Marketing and sales, two separate organizations, reported to the executive vice-president of marketing. Under marketing were the functions of market research; cost and price analysis; customer service engineering; rates, routes, and divisions; and commerce (operating authorities and other regulatory practice).

Also, the SRS adopted a program of market managers, as had a number of railroads in the 1960s. However, the relationship of the SRS market managers to the rest of the organizations of the SRS was developed in a slightly different way. On the SRS the market managers were given very narrowly defined latitude. On other railroads, the market managers were given the responsibility of selling to a specific group of shippers and being sure that the railroad profited from the activity. As discussed in chapter 2, this approach failed on most railroads because these managers were given responsibility for parts of the operation that they had no (formal or informal) authority to control. In other cases, the marketing managers on some railroads were unaware of the operating implications of what they were asking for, and operating managers found reasons why they could not comply rather than means by which to do so. At the SRS, the positive, "can-do," attitude described earlier provided a more receptive mood in the operating managers. Also, the SRS market managers were never allowed to believe that they were product managers in the sense that they could *dictate* their desires to other parts of the company. The SRS market managers had to persuade others to help them, which was possible because of the highly positive attitude just described. As it was described by one SRS executive, "the concepts of the marketing manager has to be sold to other people. He could not bull it through. He could not *make* people do anything." While placing the market manager in such a weakened position on most railroads would be fatal, it was successful on the SRS because of the spirit of integration.

Another key to the marketing success of the SRS was the premise held by operations that "controlled" (reliable) service was not necessarily more expensive to produce. This minimized the natural conflict that tends to arise between the more typical cost-minimizing operating department and the revenue-maximizing commercial departments.

Table 8-3 illustrates the effectiveness of the market managers at the SRS. In the period of 1970 through 1974, when the market managers became most effective on the SRS, several important points may be observed. Chemicals, which represented only 8.21 percent of tonnage but 12.0 percent of revenues in 1970, increased on both scores during the period. When other railroads were losing food and kindred products and farm products to owner-operater truckers, the SRS was able to increase their tonnage at some relative reduction in yield. Similar patterns may be seen in pulp and paper traffic. The SRS participated well in the transportation equipment (automobile) market until 1974. Of course, the 1974 data reflect a general deterioration of the automobile market in the United States. Perhaps the most striking point to be made is that the SRS was able to increase tonnage 9.2 percent and revenues 52.5 percent over this period, while the increase in revenue per ton mile in the Southern District was approximately 28 percent. The SRS success was on a broad front. There was little evidence that attractive traffic on the SRS was diminished. In fact, such traffic was generally increased.

One of the primary factors in the success of the SRS marketing strategy was its sensitivity to competitive threat and shipper behavior. While developing an attractive service, two other vital marketing functions were occurring on the SRS. First was the development of the cost-finding procedures described in an earlier section. Second was careful research into the alternatives the shippers had, including intermodal for-hire and private carriage, relocation, and other actions. As one SRS executive described the situation, "we know our costs and the shipper's costs and alternatives."

Table 8-3
Southern Railway System, Freight Revenue and Tonnage by Commodity Groups, 1970-1974

STCC	Commodity Group	Percent of Total Tonnage					Tons Carried (000)				
		1970	1971	1972	1973	1974	1970	1971	1972	1973	1974
1	Farm Products	4.55	4.64	4.21	4.19	4.31	6,376	6,227	6,232	6,254	6,597
10	Metallic Ores	2.22	2.33	2.10	2.09	2.12	3,110	3,127	3,108	3,130	3,250
11	Coal	25.67	24.24	25.10	23.21	24.10	36,020	32,550	37,131	34,678	36,916
14	Non-metallic minerals	11.98	11.91	12.66	12.86	12.29	16,802	15,993	18,735	19,219	18,833
20	Food and kindred products	5.86	6.00	5.70	5.92	6.07	8,217	8,066	8,434	8,847	9,293
24	Lumber and wood products	12.94	12.65	12.18	12.12	11.59	18,160	16,997	18,020	18,115	17,753
25	Furniture	0.32	0.36	0.40	0.44	0.40	450	477	587	652	616
26	Pulp and paper	5.53	5.67	5.70	6.01	6.29	7,765	7,617	8,434	8,979	9,636
28	Chemicals	8.21	8.79	8.70	9.18	9.65	11,514	11,809	12,866	13,708	14,780
29	Petroleum and coal products	2.48	2.52	2.66	2.65	2.54	3,482	3,382	3,936	3,961	3,895
32	Stone, clay, glass	8.85	8.75	9.03	9.12	8.78	12,417	11,756	13,355	13,629	13,454
33	Primary metal	3.74	3.74	3.18	3.30	3.20	5,243	5,021	4,712	4,924	4,903
34	Fabricated metal products	0.74	0.78	0.64	0.71	0.75	1,041	1,053	953	1,061	1,152
36	Electrical machinery	0.40	0.45	0.52	0.53	0.46	567	601	767	785	705
37	Transportation equipment	1.29	1.85	1.96	2.05	1.58	1,807	2,479	2,896	3,062	2,414
40	Waste and scrap	1.72	1.85	1.84	2.06	2.40	2,419	2,487	2,730	3,081	3,692
	All other	3.50	3.47	3.42	3.56	3.47	4,907	4,660	5,063	5,312	5,300
	Total carload traffic	100.00	100.00	100.00	100.00	100.00	140,297	134,302	147,959	149,397	153,189

Table 8-3 (cont.)

STCC	Commodity Group	Revenue Percent of Total					Revenue ($000)				
		1970	1971	1972	1973	1974	1970	1971	1972	1973	1974
1	Farm products	5.47	5.29	4.70	4.55	4.56	31,619	33,041	33,055	34,328	40,193
10	Metallic Ores	1.70	1.70	1.58	1.74	1.92	9,831	10,618	11,124	13,165	16,917
11	Coal	11.40	10.08	10.50	9.37	10.91	65,909	62,987	73,838	70,666	96,217
14	Non-metallic minerals	4.74	4.66	4.68	4.95	5.01	27,418	29,128	32,924	37,309	44,172
20	Food and kindred products	8.01	7.87	7.47	7.46	7.71	46,333	49,184	52,533	56,307	67,999
24	Lumber and wood products	7.79	7.67	7.94	7.99	7.57	45,046	47,907	55,843	60,245	66,782
25	Furniture	2.08	2.26	2.48	2.52	2.37	12,017	14,124	17,440	19,021	20,942
26	Pulp and paper	10.20	10.12	10.10	10.33	10.60	59,004	63,238	71,026	77,947	93,510
28	Chemicals	11.96	12.07	11.96	12.23	12.91	69,157	75,429	84,052	92,239	113,886
29	Petroluem and coal products	2.46	2.43	2.70	2.75	2.69	14,205	15,195	18,992	20,721	23,677
32	Stone, clay, glass	8.76	8.48	8.65	8.45	8.23	50,643	52,952	60,844	63,733	72,596
33	Primary metal	5.71	5.58	4.98	5.06	4.92	33,043	34,867	35,044	38,291	43,375
34	Fabricated metal products	1.79	1.81	1.48	1.61	1.65	10,363	11,327	10,415	12,134	14,583
36	Electrical machinery	1.86	1.94	2.17	2.15	1.86	10,789	12,101	15,242	16,227	16,382
37	Transportation equipment	4.77	7.02	7.39	7.63	5.88	27,595	43,868	51,940	57,566	51,858
40	Waste and scrap	2.04	2.07	2.04	2.14	2.57	11,791	12,916	14,333	16,150	22,683
	All other	9.26	8.95	9.18	9.07	8.63	53,570	55,883	64,568	68,401	76,071
	Total carload traffic	100.00	100.00	100.00	100.00	100.00	578,333	624,765	703,213	754,450	881,892

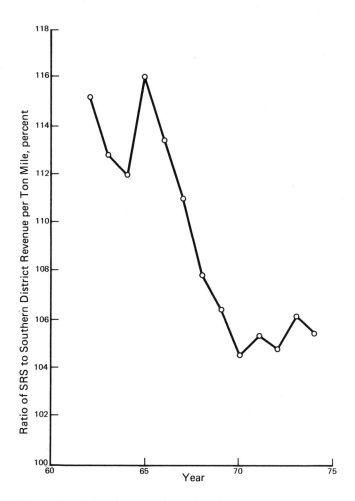

Figure 8-10. Ratio of Southern Railway System to Southern District Revenue per Ton Mile, 1962-74

While other railroads were participating in broad, across-the-board rate increases, the SRS was making selective moves with a mixture of rate reductions and increases. Special attention was devoted to the handling of some of the particularly high-yield (revenue per ton mile) traffic. As intermodal competition became more intense, the danger of losing this freight was particularly high. As the SRS became more efficient in its operations, it was possible to retain the same margins at relatively lower prices. A measure of this is the ratio of revenue per ton mile for the SRS to that of all the Southern District roads. As can be seen in figure 8-10, the SRS began to be very aggressive in this regard in the late 1960s, moving from a

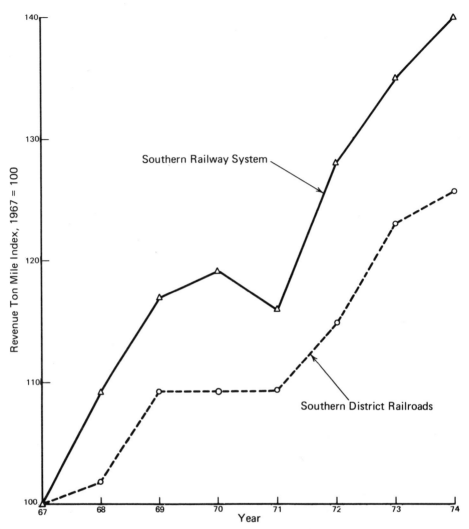

Figure 8-11. Comparison of Revenue Ton Mile Growth Rates of the Southern Railway System and All Southern District Railroads

yield premium of 12 to 16 percent down to only a 4 to 6 percent in the 1970 to 1974 period. The yield decrease was not as important as the fact that the traffic mix was retained from competitive attacks and the improving cost structure could accommodate such actions as evidenced by the stable transportation ratio and ratio of operating expenses less maintenance expenses to revenue during this same period. Here is where the vigor of operations and investment in automation and innovations coupled with excellent carrier and shipper cost finding, and aggressive stances with the ICC in a unified and integrated strategy have paid off (see figure 8-11).

Organization and Management Style

One of W.G. Claytor's major objectives upon entering the SRS was to achieve an integrated balance. One of his greatest concerns was the development of a balanced team. He went about this in several ways.

A salary review was initiated based on the assumption that certain functional areas were being compensated at higher levels than others. Consultants and a cross-functional committee undertook an objective evaluation of the entire compensation program. The contents of each position on different levels in each function were examined on the basis of several objective criteria such as level of expenditure, number of people managed, value of assets managed, visibility to the public, and potential impact on profits. After point scores were assigned, the compensation program that resulted placed the commercial and operating functions on a closer parity than had existed before. Acceptance of this notion was greatly enhanced by the extent to which operating managers had been heavy participants in the process. In fact, it was believed that a major turning point on this matter occurred when a senior operating manager on the committee found that he had objectively created a program that placed the compensation of high-ranking commercial officers above operating officers at the same level in the organizational hierarchy. The adjustment of compensation was a major signal that the commercial function was to be given full status with the operating function.

Another strong set of signals that balance and integration were to be stressed came from the creation of several cross-functional committees. In 1966 a Computer Usage Committee was created. Each functional area was represented on the committee. Its purpose was to allocate the scarce resource of computer capacity among the functions. This committee, under Claytor, developed as a working organization that members of several levels of management participated in. Individual functional groups found they had to sell the value of their programs to the common objectives to other groups. Also, a spirit of give and take between functional areas was created outside of the conventional traditions.

Another integrative organization that evolved was the Budget Committee. It was operated by the four executive vice-presidents and the comptroller (see figure 8-5). Budgets at the SRS were built from the bottom up, then reviewed at the top. The existence of detailed budgets was vital to the SRS in the exercise of control by top management. However, in the context of activities and organizations that support the integrative and vigorous spirit of the SRS, the operation of this committee had a special role. It provided the opportunity for relatively low-level management to participate in the development of the plan for the company. It forced resolution of operating and commercial conflicts at an early stage and at relatively low levels in the organization. It also served as an important training mechanism and reinforced integrative behavior.

The primary integrative mechanism and major organizational innovation of the SRS in the post-1967 period was the Management Committee. This organization, created by Claytor, was comprised of the four executive vice-presidents and the president. It met weekly and considered any area or issue in the company it desired to turn its attention to. While the four executive vice-presidents were the organizational heads of the four functional areas (operations, marketing and sales, law and finance, and administration), they were not intended to serve as the advocates for these groups in the Management Committee. Issues regarding one functional area might be brought to the attention of the committee by any other member, and in fact this was frequently the case. The individual members of the Management Committee prided themselves on their cross-functional knowledge, expertise, concern, and interest. In fact, I observed there was some evidence that the value system of the group and personal pride of the individuals emphasized this type of interfunctional behavior. Functional differentiation in the Management Committee was primarily focused on the manager's ability to serve as a resource of specific data and other detailed factual data for consideration. This was a remarkable transcendence of functional advocacy and jealousy that I had observed among managers of equal rank on other railroads.

Claytor's behavior toward this group had very significant implications for its success. First, he attempted to force resolution of interfunctional differences at the lowest possible level. A manager received no hearing on an issue if he had not already discussed the proposal with his function counterpart. Second, Claytor saw this organization as a "management committee," which he differentiated from "management by committee." As stated by Claytor, "the Management Committee has only one voting member when all is said and done." Claytor encouraged free discussion and exploration of all facets of the issue. He might ask for an indication of the sense of the Management Committee on an issue, but the final decision was his. Claytor's object was to collect all inputs from committee members. He anticipated some natural conflicts from individual functions, but he also believed that "judgement was not necessarily related to an individual's functional specialization." Another personal management style of Claytor was his questioning. When a member of the committee objects to an action, he was always pressed to articulate his reasoning, thus making it difficult to attack from emotional or traditional biases. After all discussions were completed and inputs were made, Claytor made the "decision based on the merits of the case," in the best legal tradition. To illustrate that this was not management by committee, I point to the cases where Claytor decided on a course of action that was counter to the position taken by the entire remainder of the committee. Of course, such action is unusual.

Once the decision was made, it was carried from the committee by the functional chiefs to be implemented. At this point, the SRS organization allowed no divergence. No matter what position individuals might have taken in the committee discussions, there was completely unified resolve to implement the decision fully.

Here is where the authoritarian tradition of the SRS under Brosnan may have played a role. Once the policy was set, it had to be adhered to, regardless of the specific impact it might have made on a particular functional group. However, the discipline under the Claytor administration shifted this acceptance of authority to a positive participation from the negative terror experienced in the Brosnan era. Claytor's purpose was to build a team that operated in a unified and coordinated fashion to capitalize on the tightly run, lean SRS. He felt that this philosophy of the "team" had to start from the top management and be transmitted down into the organization. The values of integrative behavior had to be reinforced by top management behavior and the normal functioning of management at all levels of the company. Claytor saw the operating rules of the railroad as "articles of war" that had to be adhered to. But, he also stressed that many decisions are best handled by good local management with good information at their disposal. He wanted to avoid "a system designed by 'headquarters geniuses' to be run by 'fools in the field.'" He wanted to develop good managers coming up through the organization. He felt that you cannot attract, retain, and develop such managements "if they don't have something to run." This attitude transmitted from the Management Committee appeared to be a major source of vigor in the organization. However, the reinforcement did not end here. It should be stressed that the SRS has a high degree of centralized (reporting) control (not necessarily direction) to assure that policies are implemented to the finest detail.

Managers at all levels in the SRS were reviewed regularly (at least annually). The review system was highly structured with the purpose of analyzing the performance of an individual and developing an action program for improvement. I reviewed the "performance analysis and recommendations," "forecast of advancement potential," and "job appraisal" forms for several SRS employees. In these records of unidentified individuals I found instances where promotions were not made because of failures to have a "broad perspective of the goals of the railroad" or "narrow parochial attitudes." While the number of instances of this I observed were few, this attitude was well-known by the employees of the SRS. I was unable to find evidence of such behavior on the other railroads where I conducted such research.

Among the attitude questionnaires completed by SRS managers (see chapter 6), the average priority assigned to improved coordination of the marketing and operations function was only 6.5 out of 7. Clearly, the managers at all levels of the SRS perceive that this is not a serious problem in their company.

Conclusions

The SRS has had an unusual recent history. The circumstances it found itself in for the past several years are not necessarily directly comparable to other railroads. Thus, the specific actions of the SRS are probably not appropriate for other railroads. My selection of the SRS for a detailed description and discussion is intended primarily to illustrate a pattern of development and innovation in management style and organization in the spirit of contingency management theory.

The pre-1967 era was a period of tightening of operations on the SRS. Authoritarian and dictatorial management in an ambiguously defined organization structure was consistent with a period of rapidly introduced operating innovations. Greater rigidity of organization would have constricted this innovation. The failure of Brosnan to achieve this structure probably saved the SRS from greater centralization and was perhaps a major factor at that stage in maintaining vigor in a local level where a high degree of detailed finesse in operations can occur. For it is at this level of detail that information exists. To accommodate this situation, systems were designed to communicate system data and policies to these lower decision-making levels. By this improbable and awkward process, the SRS fortunately maintained local vigor, and actually supplemented it in a highly disciplined fashion. While Brosnan could understand the need for greater integration of the operating and commercial functions, his own experiences and personality prevented him from making the adjustments necessary to fully achieve a balanced and integrated attack on the problem of developing traffic. He took the steps that tightened operations and started the marketing philosophy of the company, but he could shift to a more disciplined and integrative mode of behavior.

Claytor was the president for the new strategy of building the business on the operating foundations established by Brosnan. He went beyond Brosnan's earlier attempts at recognition of the status of the marketing function as a full equal operation. The innovations of the Management Committee and other integrative committees, adjusted compensation programs, and reward-punishment system recognizing integrative behavior,

vigorous initiative, and innovation became the improbable but successful surrogate for the more conventional, but less feasible in the railroad industry, decentralized, profit-center methods.
recognizing integrative behavior, vigorous initiative, and innovation became the improbable but successful surrogate for the more conventional, but less feasible in the railroad industry, decentralized, profit-center methods.

But, as one SRS executive expressed it, "we all realize you can't operate a railroad as a *group* of profit centers. A railroad is an interrelated system and must function as a system if it is going to be profitable.[2]

The SRS achieved vigor and an innovativeness at all levels of management the "hard way," compared to the means available in more businesses that are readily divisionalized into clearly identified profit centers. The Southern Railroad System experience demonstrates that these goals can be accomplished with diligence and energy. The SRS strategy was a combination of alternatives 3, 4, and 6 analyzed in chapter 7. While the SRS was successful in achieving these goals, and it may be the only satisfactory approach to restored vigor and integration on railroads, I would still call it the "improbable solution" because most managers on other railroads may not have the financial and middle management resources available to them in sufficient quantity to help their companies soon enough to save them.

Notes

1 "The Five Best-Managed Companies," *Dun's Review,* December 1974, pp. 46-51.
2 "Cars, Computers, and Cash Flow," *Transportation and Distribution Management,* September-October 1974, pp. 53-58.

9 Concluding Remarks

The plight of railroads in the United States is not hopeless, but this may not be true much longer. With each passing year of inaction the fate of the railroads (i.e., nationalization) is becoming more certain. A general lack of appreciation for the nature of the organizational failing of railroads has led the United States government to undertake a well-intended but disastrous step in the formation of the quasi-public Conrail organization. Conrail merged several railroads that had been unmanageable with conventional railroad management styles and organization because of their size. Creating larger units that are less manageable is hardly a solution.

The performance of railroad organization has been poor. There is clear evidence that major sources of the failure of railroads are the organization and management style that have evolved as "standard" or conventional among railroads of the United States. Railroad organizations have promoted continued, competitively insulated, "monopoly thinking" in an increasingly intermodal competitive environment. Similarly they have promoted dysfunctional differentiation, particularly undercutting marketing, when they most required functional integration for a unified, competitive response. The conventional railroad organizations have failed to generate vigorous local management in a highly transaction-oriented operation with substantial local demands.

Railroads were the first great organizational innovators of the nineteenth century. The adaptive thinking and organizational creativity of the railroads of that period were the first examples of the contingency management theory. But in the twentieth century stagnation occurred. Organizational adaptiveness, for all practical purposes, ended in the first quarter of the century. Railroads must regain this organizational innovativeness; they must look at themselves in a new light. There is a variable that is within the control of management organization, its structure, and its use. The goals should be increased vigor and aggressiveness at all levels, and integration of functions into a unified, competitive attack at all levels. The technology, traditions, regulations, and other features of the industry make this a difficult task; if it were not difficult, it would have been accomplished before now. The challenge is to reexamine the issues and alternatives. Several railroads have broken out of the pack to do it, and some remarkable results are already being seen for these efforts.

171

Performance of Organizations and Managers

There is evidence that railroad middle managers may not have as much formal training as their counterparts in organizations of equivalent size. But, there is no evidence that these managers have any less native intelligence or management potential. It is conventional wisdom that railroad managers are older than their counterparts in other industries. But, examination of railroad management did not support this. In fact, railroad managers are not appreciably different from their counterparts in firms of similar size. If anything, the average age of top managers in railroads may be lowering.

If there is a failing of railroad management, the failure is more with the system of development and organization than with the managers. Of course, one might say that very strong managers would overcome these problems. However, this may be asking a great deal of the average manager.

There is disparity between the orientations of the individual, differentiated functional groups of railroads. As might be expected, operating managers were substantially more interested in operations, blaming low labor productivity on restrictive labor agreements, and blaming the lack of profitable traffic on pricing problems. The marketing managers wanted greater resources devoted to selling and developing a lower priced service. The greatest disparity in attitudes found was the perception needs for improved coordination between the operating and commercial functions. Operating managers saw little need, while commercial (or marketing) and administrative managers saw this as one of the highest priorities for improvement on their railroads. This breakdown is of importance when the balance of power of railroads is considered. Clearly, operations is still the group with the clout, and operations appears to have little perception of or intention of acting on the coordination problems. Therefore, there is little likelihood that this is a self-correcting situation. If greater coordination occurs, it will be because of a strong-minded, conscious effort to counteract prevailing forces on railroads.

There is further evidence that this will not come about easily. There is greater functional differentiation among top managers than middle managers of individual functions. Indeed, this dysfunctional behavior may be transmitted down into the organization. So, there is substantial need to redirect the attitudes of many top managers to promote integration rather than condone or promote functional jealousy.

This is a problem that appears to be a typical occurrence in most large organizations with highly differentiated functional departments. In this regard, railroads and their managers are following patterns observed in other industries and some (particularly large) bureaucracies. But, that does not make it desirable or acceptable for this industry.

The conventional form of organization found on nearly every railroad in the United States has not demonstrated that it is particularly suitable for managing a large number of transactions on a large geographically dispersed system. As the scale of the operation increases, the transportation expenses deteriorate rapidly. Only in railroads of longer average length of haul, where the intercity portion of the revenues was substantial, could this problem be concealed. In the past two decades, railroads have typically attempted to use the computer and electronic data processing to centralize control. Rather than help this situation, it has hurt. The railroads were pushing the computer to perform functions that were better performed by good local managers aided by better system information. Investment in automated yards gave managers a false sense that they were relieved of minimizing yard involvement.

False confidence has been placed in computers and the wisdom of central wizards. Undercutting the role of the local manager has led to the loss of vigor at the very point in the organization where it is needed most, where the operations physically occur. As all of these errors were being committed, the financial community and ICC, encouraged by government, have continued on the course of creating larger and more unmanageable railroad enterprises. Their desires for consolidating firms to reduce redundancy and interline exchanges were worthy, but the premise that the railroads had the management technology and organizations to support such consolidations was faulty. The redundancies were often not rationalized and the unexpected diseconomics of scale were a bitter price to pay.

Many of the railroads of the United States are of unmanageable size, given the management styles and organizations that they are presently committed to, and to add to the problem, the present concept of Conrail and further merger of railroads without correction of this problem will only aggravate this already unfortunate situation.

Previous Appropriations Leading to Stagnation

The railroads of the United States were the first major enterprises to experiment with new organizational forms for managing large-scale operations. The nineteenth century was a period of great creativity and flexibility in railroad organizaions. But a series of events changed this after the beginning of the twentieth century. A sense of self-satisfaction and a belief that the *one appropriate organization* had evolved appears to have set in at this point. Regulation stabilized competition and the lack of intermodal competition led to little concern for marketing and a concentration on operations. With inflation and regulated rates, there was a natural tendency to focus on cost reduction, leading railroads to produce a less-desirable service at a lower cost, after ignoring the desires of shippers and what was occurring in the competitive environment.

Regulation of railroads by the ICC may be condemned on several counts. But, two of the most damaging and subtle of these have been (1) the false sense of isolation from the environment, and (2) the sense of timidness for regarding innovation that the ICC has engendered among the railroads.

The stagnation has been aggravated by the high degree of on-the-job training, promotion from within the company and industry, and de facto seniority systems of the railroad industry. All of these features have substantially reduced innovativeness and flexibility, reinforced old values, and rewarded "patient waiting" rather than vigorous and aggressive attack. This brings us to the present and raises the question, what courses are open to the railroads?

What Next?

How can railroads increase vigor and aggressiveness and integration at all levels of their organizations? The forces working against the achievement of these objectives are substantial.

The basic systemic and joint-produce nature of railroad operations generally precludes extensive use of profit-center accountability, the conventional tool of decentralization of integrative behavior in other industries. The traditional operating orientation of railroads' top managers tends to insulate them from an awareness of the need for or the capability of achieving a greater balance between the operating and marketing functions. This is particularly serious since the effective integration of the commercial function is probably the primary key to the survival of the railroads in the highly competitive intermodal arena. The disparity between the views of the large number of railroad middle managers and their top managers suggests that the leaders of railroads are not particularly effective in controlling the thinking of the subordinates. This may be very fortunate because some of the middle managers may not be as set in their functional biases as their leaders are.

The hope for railroads appears to lie in a shift in the attitudes of the leadership of railroads. Top management must be the fountainhead of integration rather than the source of dysfunctional-functional jealousies. In turn, signals must be communicated that integrative behavior is rewarded rather than seen as a sign of weakness in subordinates. This has been accomplished on one railroad. However, to do this it took a group of highly secure and confident managers, a conscious effort to overcome natural tendencies toward differentiation, and a balancing of the power bases of the separate functional groups. While it is not typically the easier method to achieve integration in conventional enterprises, it has been demonstrated that it is possible to stimulate integration from the top down. Given the constraints described above, this may be the *only* practical means to achieve the objective of integration throughout a railroad for a unified, competitive response.

Railroads must increasingly be concerned with the transactional content of their operations; they must turn management attention either to transactions or to getting competent management where transactions occur.

Only at the local level is there sufficient information to achieve transactional finesse. Restoring or increasing local aggressiveness on railroads is a major task because it requires a substantial change in the attitudes of top management toward local managers. It requires modification of the present philosophy that local aggressiveness may be sacrificed for the potential of system optimization. It suggests that greater autonomy be given to the local manager, but it also implies establishing performance guidelines and objectives, monitoring performance, and supplementing local decision making with better data and knowledge of the implications of local decisions on the system.

Railroad management must recognize that transactions are a major cause of diseconomies of scale in railroading. While electronic data processing has had some potential for reducing this impact, it has tended to kill the vigor of local management because of the way the computer has been applied. Avoidance of yards, even if automated, and minimization of tranactions, even if computerized, must be followed as guiding principles.

Assembly of larger railroad enterprises must be prevented, unless management styles and organizations substantially more effective in handling transactions are implemented or the merger reduces transactions (i.e., eliminates interlining).

In summary, the tasks before the railroads are relatively simple to state but difficult to accomplish.

1. Balance of power of the functional groups
2. Integration of the functional groups at *all* levels of the organization, particularly at the top
3. Well-trained and competent middle management capable of vigorous and aggressive decentralized operations

The objectives can still be accomplished in several ways. But, the means of doing so are rapidly being closed by managements' failure to act and governments' willingness to act. The opportunity exists; will management accept the challenge? It was once stated, "God made the World in 4004 B.C., but it was reorganized in 1901 by James J. Hill, J. Pierpont Morgan and John D. Rockefeller."[1] It is long past the time to reorganize the world that Hill, Morgan, and Rockefeller left for the United States railroads.

Note

1. *Life Magazine*, January 24, 1901.

Glossary

Automatic Block Control. System of signals that automatically indicates to trains about to enter a segment of track whether it is occupied by another train.

Bad Order. Car or locomotive needing repairs.

Balkanization. A condition in which individual railroads find themselves at once dependent upon competitors for survival.

Ballast. The material placed on the roadbed beneath and around the crossties to hold the track in place.

Bill of Lading. Form of contract between the shippers and the carrier specifying the details of routing, consignor, consignee, commodity, and special terms and conditions or instructions.

Blind Track. A block of track with no signalling on which operations are controlled by a system of written procedures and special train orders.

Block. A length of track of defined limits, the use of which by trains and engines is governed by block signals, cab signals, or both.

Carload. (a) Quantity of freight required to fill a rail car; (b) the quantity of freight necessary to qualify a shipment for a carload rate.

Car Man. Mechanical repairman or inspector of railroad rolling stock.

Centralized Traffic Control. A system to control the movement of trains by means of remotely controlled signals and switches from a central location by a dispatcher.

Class I Railroads. Railroads with average gross operating revenues of $3 million or more annually from railroad operations (prior to 1974, more than $1 million).

COFC. Container on flat car.

Commodity. Any article of commerce; goods shipped.

Conductor. In charge of the train. He is responsible for the freight carried in the cars of the train. He is to check to see that cars are dropped or set out at the proper points and see that empty or loaded cars are picked up.

Consignee. The terminator of a shipment.

Consignor. The originator of a shipment.

Crossties. The wooden, concrete, or steel crosspieces that support the rails in the track.

Dispatcher. Issues orders for the operation of a train. Controls the movements of trains in various sections of the railroad. Generally reports to a division superintendent.

Division. That portion of a railroad typically assigned to the supervision of a superintendent.

Division Point. The point at which a train crew is relieved.

Doubling Over. Assembling strings of cars from two or more tracks in a yard.

Engine. A unit propelled by any form of energy, or a combination of such units operated from a single control.

Engineer. The operator of the locomotive.

Enroute. On the way.

Fireman. Aids the engineer in the operation of the locomotive.

Flat Switch Yard. A yard in which switching is performed with a locomotive rather than gravity (as in a hump yard).

Foreign Car. Car from another railroad.

Freight Bill. Document from a common carrier shipment. Gives description of the freight, its weight, amount of charges, taxes, and whether collect or prepaid. Charges paid in advance are called *prepaid freight bills*. Charges collected at the destination are called *destination* or *collect freight bills*.

General Operating Expenses. Generally similar to general and administrative expenses in conventional accounting.

Hump Yard. A yard in which switching is performed by gravity. Cars are pushed over an elevated piece of track and allowed to roll into individual tracks to be joined with other cars for the same destination or area.

Industry Switching. The operation of local pickup and delivery of railroad cars.

Interstate Commerce Act. An act of Congress regulating the practice, rates, and rules of transportation lines engaged in hauling interstate traffic.

Interstate Commerce Commission (ICC). The federal body charged with enforcing acts of Congress affecting interstate commerce.

Interline Freight. Freight that moves from point of origin to destination over the line of two or more transportation companies.

Main Track. A track extending through yards and between stations, upon which trains are operated by timetable or train order, or both, or the use of which is governed by block signals.

Maintenance of Equipment. Repair and depreciation of rolling stock.

Maintenance of Way and Structure. Repair and depreciation of roadway.

Owner-Operator. A truck owner and operator. Usually a single truck operator in truckload operations, frequently in competition with railroads.

Per Diem. The charge made per day between railroads for foreign cars.

PICL. Perpetual Inventory of Car Location: a system for maintaining inventory of railroad cars in yards. The system uses a punch card, which is created for each car when it enters the yard. A set of slots representing individual yard tracks serves as a model of the yard. Cards representing cars are moved from one slot to another reflecting car movements in the yard.

Piggy Back. An intermodal form of transportation where trailers or containers are carried by rail and truck. TOFC.

Point of Origin. The point at which freight is received from the shipper.

Rate. The charge for transporting freight.

Right of Way. The land upon which the railroad is built.

Roadway. The structure supporting and forming the railroad track.

Schedule. That part of a timetable that prescribes class, direction, number, and movement for regular trains.

Set Out. The act of dropping rail cars from an enroute train.

Shipper. The individual or institution that pays for the shipment. This may be the consignor, consignee, or a third party.

Siding. A track auxiliary to the main track for meeting or passing trains.

Slow Order. An order to train crews restricting the speed of operations.

Station. A place designated on the timetable by name.

Switch. Connection between two lines of track to permit cars or trains to pass from one track to another.

Switch List. Document listing instructions for picking up, delivering, or otherwise locating or assembling equipment by a switch crew.

Timetable. The authority for the movement of regular trains subject to the rules and special instructions.

TOFC. Trailer on flat car.

Train. An engine or engines with or without cars, displaying markers.

Train Master. Direct train and switching operations in terminals, stations, and yards. Generally reports to a division superintendent.

Transportation. The portion of railroad operations generally related to the movement of trains.

Transportation Expenses. The expenses directly associated with the transportation operations of a railroad. They generally include the expenses of crews, fuel, and other related items.

Waybill. Description of goods sent with a common carrier freight shipment.

Yard. A system of tracks within defined limits, over which movements may be made subject to prescribed signals and rules, or special instructions.

Bibliography

General Management

Lawrence, Paul, and Jay Lorsch, *Organization and Environment, Managing Differentiation and Integration* (Boston: Division of Research, Harvard Business School, 1967).

President Profile: Bank and Bank Holding Company (New York: Heidrick and Struggles, 1974).

Profile of a Chief Financial Officer (New York: Heidrick and Struggles, 1970).

Profile of a Chief Marketing Executive (New York: Heidrick and Struggles, 1971).

Profile of a Chief Research and Development Executive (New York: Heidrick and Struggles, 1973).

"Selling Compensation," *Sales Management*, January 6, 1975, pp. 44-51.

White, William H., Jr., *The Organization Man* (Garden City, New York: Doubleday and Co., Inc., 1956).

Wyckoff, D. Daryl, *Organizational Formality and Performance in the Motor-Carrier Industry* (Lexington, Mass.: Lexington Books, D.C. Heath and Company, 1974).

Wyckoff, D. Daryl, and David H. Maister, *The Owner-Operator: Independent Trucker* (Lexington, Mass.: Lexington Books, D.C. Heath Company, 1975).

Historical Railroads—United States

Athern, Robert G., *Union Pacific Country* (Chicago: Rand McNally and Company, 1971).

Brandeis, Louis D., *Scientific Management and Railroads* (New York: The Engineering Magazine, 1911).

Bryant, Keith L., Jr., *History of the Atchison, Topeka, and Santa Fe Railway* (New York: Macmillan, Inc., 1974).

Chandler, Alfred D., *Henry Varnum Poor: Business Editor, Analyst, and Reformer* (Cambridge, Mass.: Harvard University Press, 1956).

_____. "The Railroads: Pioneers in Modern Corporate Management," *Business History Review*, Spring 1965, pp. 16-39.

_____. *The Railroads—The Nation's First Big Business* (New York: Harcourt, Brace & World, Inc., 1965).

Cochran, Thomas. C., *Railroad Leaders 1845-1890: The Business Mind in Action* (Cambridge, Mass.: Harvard University Press, 1953).

Cordeal, Ernest, *Railroad Operation* (New York: Simmons-Boardman Publishing Company, 1924).

Derleth, August W., *The Milwaukee Road: Its First Hundred Years* (New York: Creative Age Press, 1948).

Illinois Central Research and Development Bureau, ed., *Organization and Traffic of the Illinois Central System* (Chicago: Illinois Central Railroad Company, 1938).

Joy, Stewart, *The Train that Ran Away* (London: Ian Allan Ltd., 1973).

Lee, Ivy L., *Human Nature and Railroads* (Philadelphia: E.S. Nash and Co., 1915).

Mazlish, Bruce, ed., *The Railroad and the Space Program* (Cambridge, Mass.: The M.I.T. Press, 1965).

McCallum, Daniel C., "Superintendent's Report," *Annual Report of the New York and Erie Railroad Company for 1855* (New York, 1856).

McPherson, Logan G. *The Working of the Railroads* (New York: Henry Holt and Company, 1907).

Morris, Stuart, "Stalled Professionalism: The Recruitment of Railway Officials in the United States, 1885-1940," *Business History Review*, Autumn 1973, pp. 317-34.

O'Connor, Richard, *Iron Wheels and Broken Men* (New York: Putnam, 1973).

Peabody, James, *Railway Organization and Management* (Chicago, La Salle Extension University, 1916).

Priestley, Neville, *Organization and Working of Railways in America* (London: Eyre and Spottiswoode, 1904).

Nichols, Clarence E. *Standard Railroad Textbook* (Portland, Oregon: Railroad Textbook Co., Inc., 1941).

Sharfman, I. Leo, *The American Railroad Problem* (New York: The Century Co., 1921).

Sobel, Robert, *The Entrepreneurs* (New York: Weybright and Talley, 1974), particularly chap. IV, "James J. Hill: The Business of Empire."

Stover, John F., *American Railroads* (Chicago: The University of Chicago Press, 1961).

Vanderblue, H.B., and K.F. Burgess, *Railroads: Rates, Service Management* (New York: Macmillan, Inc., 1924).

"When the U.S. Took Over the Railroads," *Railroad Magazine*, October 1938.

Historical Railroads—United Kingdom

Gournish, Terence R., "A British Business Elite: The Chief Executive Managers of the Railway Industry, 1850-1922," *Business History Review*, Autumn 1973, pp. 289-316.

———., *Mark Huish and the London and North Western Railway: A Study of Management* (Leicester: Leicester University Press, 1972).

Simmons, Jack, *The Railways of Britain* (New York: Macmillan, Inc. 1968).

Railroad Management

Bronson, Gail, "More Disgruntled Shippers Underwrite Routine Railroad Maintenance Inspection," *Wall Street Journal*, October 16, 1974.

Chesser, A.H., "To Our Mutual Advantage," *Handling and Shipping* (President's Issue), 1972.

Cottrell, W. Fredrick, *The Railroader* (Stanford, Calif.: Stanford University Press, 1940).

———, *Technological Change and Labor in the Railroad Industry* (Lexington, Mass.: Lexington Books, D.C. Heath and Company, 1970).

"Decision Makers 1974" *Modern Railroads,* October 1974.

Dick, Merwin, "Making Bad Track Good: What are the Economics?" *Railway Age*, June 9, 1975, p. 36.

Ford, Nancy, "The Customer Speaks," *Modern Railroads,* November 1974.

———, "Do We Really Understand Marketing?" *Modern Railroads,* August 1972, pp. 26-31.

Healy, Kent T., *The Effects of Scale in the Railroad Industry* (New Haven, Conn.: Yale University, 1961).

Healy, Patrick T., and Alexander L. Morton, *Note on Train Scheduling and Operating Procedures* (Boston: Harvard Business School, 1974).

Improving Railroad Productivity (Washington, D.C.: National Commission on Productivity, 1973).

Lapp, Charles J., "An Empirical Study of Some Relationships Between Technological Innovations and Organizational Characteristics in Eight Railroads" (Evanston, Ill.: Northwestern University, Masters of Science Thesis, 1966).

Levitt, Theodore, *Innovation in Marketing* (New York: McGraw-Hill Book Company, Inc., 1962).

McCue, Michael, and W.A. Pinkerton, *Comparative Note on Freight Car Management* (Boston: Harvard Business School, 1974).

186

Morton, Alexander L., "Balkanization in the Railroad Industry," *Proceedings of the Transportation Research Forum*, 1974, pp. 14-17.

Meyer, John R., and Alexander L. Morton, "A Better Way to Run the Railroads," *Harvard Business Review*, July-August 1974, pp. 141-48.

Meyers, Edward T., "The Cancer of Maintenance Deferral," *Modern Railroads*, March 1974.

————., "Repair to Meet the Future," *Modern Railroads*, March 1974.

Paul, Bill, "Federal Effort to Reduce Rail Accidents is a Bust; Many Factors Share the Blame," *Wall Street Journal*, October 21, 1974.

Phelps, Lewis M., "As Railroads Defer More Maintenance, Number of Accidents Increases Sharply," *Wall Street Journal*, October 10, 1974.

Shaffer, Frank E., "Taking Car Utilization to Task," *Modern Railroads*, July 1975, pp. 56-58.

U.S. Presidential Railroad Commission, *Report of the Presidential Railroad Commission* (Washington, D.C.: 1962).

Index

Index

About the Author

D. Daryl Wyckoff is an associate professor at the Harvard University Graduate School of Business Administration, George F. Baker Foundation. He received the B.S. in aeronautical engineering from M.I.T., the M.B.A. from the University of Southern California, and the D.B.A. from Harvard University. In the past he has served as the vice president of the logistics systems group of a California based aerospace conglomerate and he continues to serve as a consultant in management, transportation, and logistics to companies, governments, and industry organizations in the United States, United Kingdom, and several countries in the Middle East. Dr. Wyckoff is the author of *Organizational Formality and Performance in the Motor Carrier Industry* (Lexington Books, 1974), and is coauthor of *The Owner-Operator: Independent Trucker* (Lexington Books, 1975), and *Operations Management: Text and Cases* (Richard D. Irwin, 1975). His articles have appeared in *Traffic World*, *Modern Railroads*, *Handling and Shipping,* and *Transportation and Distribution Management*.

CANCE